Murder and Misunderstanding

One Man's Escape from Insanity

Shubi S.

Surinder LLC
Lancaster, PA

Surinder LLC
Lancaster, PA 17601

Copyright © 2012 by Shuvender Sem

All rights reserved. No part of this book may be reproduced in any form or by any electronic or mechanical means, including information storage and retrieval systems, without written permission from the publisher or author, except in the case of a reviewer, who may quote brief passages embodied in critical articles or in a review.

Cover design by Green Vine Marketing

First Edition
ISBN-13: 978-1479256969
ISBN-10: 147925696X
Printed in the United States of America

Shubi S.

Foreword

When people think about schizophrenia, scary images of dirty, homeless beggars often come to mind.

A word of warning: this book isn't going to completely alleviate that perception.

As I tell my story, years of psychotropic medications have indeed taken their toll. But for the most part, I have a pretty good memory of things - a "sanely insane" awareness is what I like to call it.

Paranoid Schizophrenia has always been "the crazy man's disease." You hear the silent voices in your head, you are extremely paranoid … it is the epitome of someone who has lost touch with reality. Indeed such statements are true, but the demonization of those suffering with it implies they are evil and corrupt when in reality they are just ill. And despite what it may seem, the truth remains that individuals with schizophrenia are real people from real families with real lives, just like everyone else.

I'm a perfect example: a normal kid who grew up in the suburbs with the house, the dog, the family business and the education - who just *happened* to also be challenged with paranoid schizophrenia …

But there's something more.

I want to demystify the stigma that comes with this disease and let people see the human side of it, possibly giving hope to those who suffer with it endlessly. Don't believe what you've heard. It isn't automatically a death sentence. I don't know how I made it through those dark years, but I did. And I want people to know - whether they have a mental illness or a family member or friend suffering with it - that they too can live a normal life - even after hitting rock bottom. And the bottom doesn't get any rockier than mine.

When I decided to write this book, my intention was to tell the story of my journey with mental illness. I envisioned the many people I would help in some way. Perhaps the health care system would be impacted enough to change their treatment of its mentally ill by people like me speaking out ...

Or perhaps law enforcement would be inspired to learn more about diseases like paranoid schizophrenia so they would be better equipped to handle incidents with a person having delusions...

The one thing I didn't anticipate was what this book would do for my own salvation.

Along with a steadfast diet of psychotherapy, this authoring experience has shown me that my story never began with me, it always began with my father. And as time went on, as I began to write about my father, I came to realize who he was ... and who I was, too.

For way too long I thought he was the reason for my troubles in life. I loved him, I hated him, I needed him ... and I resented him. I so wanted his love in a way I could comprehend that it ended up leading me on many paths trying to find it.

Initially, this book was about those paths and my quest for his love and approval. But as I continued to write my story those paths became less foggy and more clear. It enabled me to step back and view my life more objectively, giving me the opportunity to see where I had made my own choices and how the ones I didn't have as much control over taught me great lessons and built my character.

All in all, the creative process of publishing this book has brought me full circle, back to where I belong - a place where I accept my father and, more importantly, a place where I accept myself.

Shubi S.

I dedicate this book to him - my dad - *The Man, The Undercover Sailkot Indian Artist* ... and to all the people who live with this illness. May the world be better after this book than before.

1

The Undercover Indian Artist

Dad fought hard to keep the tears away as his heart broke in two. He was only fifteen years old. It was India, 1952 ... and the woman who had birthed him was gone.

He remembers the pain and disbelief of his mother's sudden demise. Insisting she was still alive and that she would suffocate, Dad resisted his father as he tried to drape the cloth over her face. Finally, the reality that she was no longer in her body sank in and he watched somberly as the men carried her away. Relatives were called and she was cremated - as was traditionally practiced in Hindu custom.

The air was cold as he forged his way over to the well to draw water the next day. It was an interesting place to be, considering his soul had run dry and needed replenishment. Dad had much to contemplate as his life shifted meaning. Now, as he stretched his back and arms, pulling on the ropes in a motion to bring the wooden bucket up to the surface, he had a new purpose: caring for his five younger brothers and sisters. His mother did everything. Someone had to step up and fill the void somehow. And although the sadness seemed never-ending, there was no other choice but to move on.

Dad was born in *Sailkot*, India in 1937, the second-oldest son of seven children. He had one older brother, three younger brothers and two younger sisters. His childhood occurred during a time of severe social upheaval. In 1947, when Dad was 10, two significant events occurred. One, India achieved its independence from the British Empire, resulting in the Muslim residents of Pathankot, Gurdaspur and other parts of East Punjab moving into Sailkot as refugees to settle there. And two, what became known as the Great Partition of India took place.

The country was in an uproar. Political forces, after months of conflict and negotiations, legally split the land. As a result, Pakistan was born. Two separate pieces of land became the new country, but they were on opposite sides of India. East Pakistan (today Bangladesh) and West Pakistan were separated geographically by India. The region became divided between the majority Hindu areas (British India) and the majority Muslim areas (Pakistan).

Aside from his mother's death, which would come five years later, this was Dad's most salient childhood memory: the day he and his family had to leave their home. When the *Partition of India* took place and the country was divided, my dad's family had to leave everything behind to relocate. This was not a choice. Sailkot became part of Pakistan which was majority Muslim. My family is Hindu. Remaining in a place designated for Muslims was too dangerous.

Painfully, and against their will, my grandparents closed down their business, packed what they could carry, and embarked on the journey to India with their seven children in tow. It was a long voyage made on foot - no Amtrak, Delta Airlines or car pooling was available.

This was a dislocation, with hundreds of thousands of people on their way to nowhere in particular. Dad's family was one of the luckier ones. His father had a brother who lived in the capital of India at the time and offered a place for the family to stay.

In their new surroundings, the quality of life was not as good as what they once enjoyed. The house they shared was small and the city was congested. But life had to go on - that is, until my grandmother's nose began bleeding suddenly. She was always a very busy woman. If she wasn't doing laundry, she was cooking. If she wasn't preparing food, she was cleaning. And if she wasn't cleaning, she was taking care of the children. A strong-willed woman who never complained and never sat still, it took the blood suddenly streaming from her nose to snag everyone's attention. A red flag went off. My father rushed to her side as she stumbled to the floor.

Shocked, Dad didn't know what to do except hold her and ask what was wrong. She was always the strong one. Now suddenly he found himself supporting her - a new role that was strange and uncomfortable to him. As she laid there in his arms, losing consciousness, her soul slipping away, Dad could only be a dependent witness. In a few moments she would be gone … and he would be left asking the question: why did this happen?

In that place and time, annual doctor check-ups were unheard of. For the most part, if you couldn't fix something with home remedies, then you just sucked it up and kept moving. It turned out that his mother's cause of death was linked to high blood pressure that had gone untreated for too long. No one knew - not even his mother - until it was too late.

With the matriarch gone, things in the family began to slowly unravel. Dad's older brother, my uncle, didn't see eye to eye with their father and it wasn't long before my uncle moved out to be on his own, leaving Dad as the eldest son of the house for his remaining teenage years.

After his eighteenth birthday, he enrolled in the local university. Dad was passionate about history and immersed himself in the school curriculum as a History major.

In 1962, when Dad was 25 years old, the Sino-Indian War broke out. Young men were signing up for battle. There were no drafts in India. Men considered it an honor to serve their country in such a manner. Dad was no exception. He filled out the paperwork and received the position of colonel. Soon after, he and his squad were assigned to border patrol at *Nathu La* - a mountain pass in the Himalayas and a border cross between *Tibet* in China and *Sikkim* in India. After the People's Republic of China took control of *Tibet* in 1950, the passes into *Sikkim* became a conduit for refugees from *Tibet*, leaving *Nathu La* ripe for skirmishes between soldiers of the two countries. It was also a prime site for military protection, since the opening shortened the travel distance to important Hindu and Buddhist pilgrimage sites in the region.

It was common for Dad and his fellow troops to have border conflicts with China's *People's Liberation Army*. Snipers aimed from afar and the guys had to stay on their toes - which wasn't difficult to do, considering the freezing cold of the Himalayan's snow-capped mountains.

My father recalls nights huddled around a crackling fire with a brigade of soldiers. After a long day, the look in the eyes of his fellow soldiers sang the song of many sorrows and fears unable to be expressed between men. The Himalayan wind would whistle through the caverns and the "kaw" of the hawks echoing in the distance made it seem like they were a million miles away from the rest of the world.

The pressure of protecting the border cross for the safety of their country was heavy in the air, so my father would sing for them. He was an undercover artist at heart, but a soldier by day. His soul was only truly soothed by creative expression – at this time in his life, mainly singing. The melodies he created also made being away from home and in daily peril a little less harrowing - at least for the moment. At worst it reminded the men of what was normal; at best it brought in a little piece of something familiar. War was the opposite of normal. Soldiers were usually nostalgic for whatever would remind them of life before soldiering.

During this time, one of Dad's best friends got married back home and he was, of course, invited to be there. In fact, he looked forward to it. The war was beginning to take its toll - especially on someone as fun-loving as he was. Eager to get away, Dad happily signed up for a weekend pass. At the wedding, he was introduced to his friend's new bride after the rituals were over. Next to her stood the woman who would forever steal his heart - my mother. The bride was her cousin and Mom was there to support her. As the story goes, she "had dad at hello." But Mom was a woman who thought with her head more than her heart. Though love was instant for my Dad, the romantic free-spirit, it was an intellectual decision for my mother. She needed to think about what a relationship would be and whether or not they were compatible. At the time, Dad was in the army and Mom was getting her education, so she was in no hurry to be married anyway.

In 1975, *Sikkim* acceded to India and *Nathu La* became part of Indian territory. China, however, refused to acknowledge the accession, continuing the need for border patrol. However, by this time, Dad was no longer in the service, having finished his five year term in 1967. Honored to have had the opportunity to serve his country, Dad recognized that his time was up. A young man turning thirty, he had his whole life to live. Besides, he was in love and his future was somewhere else, not with the military.

In 1967 when Dad arrived back home, the house was caught in a whirlwind of family drama. His uncle, who apprenticed with his father for many years, had decided to open his own photography business in the same neighborhood. The store was close enough to cause a "Starbucks versus the local coffee shop" battle for survival. It was an unforeseen stab in the back since Dad's father had taught this uncle, his own brother, everything he knew. It also seemed that Dad's uncle kept his plans to open his own business a secret, which added to the sting of the betrayal. Dad walked into a heated family debate over the issue. His father was not a spring chicken anymore and didn't have the fight in him like he used to. My grandfather, like my father, also was the sibling who looked out for the others and always made sure they were taken care of.

"So this is how you treat him?" Dad was confronting his uncle in his new store, furious. "All he has done for you and your family and he is rewarded by you putting him out of business?" He had never spoken to his uncle like this before, as it was against custom to confront your elders, but something had to be done. In India, it was a communal culture. Family was everything - the central core. Dishonor could not be tolerated. It was hard enough trying to survive as a unit during those times, but a family divided simply would not stand.

Despite the repercussions, Dad's uncle remained determined to keep running his business, ultimately causing a riff within the family. With his one older brother still out in the world forsaking the duty as the eldest child, Dad was left to reclaim the responsibility of looking out for his younger siblings once again.

Amidst his eldest son being estranged, his second eldest son being off at war, having five more children at home and the above family turmoil, my grandfather had also taken himself a new wife. Some time had passed since my grandmother's death and my grandfather was longing for companionship again. Culturally, the woman was the nucleus that held the household together. With circumstances being as they were the need for a woman became very non-optional. Years had come and gone since grandmother's sudden passing, and Dad's two sisters had become accustomed to picking up the slack their mother had left. In essence, they were the women of the house when their father introduced his new bride. They did not like her and apparently the feelings were mutual. It

Murder and Misunderstanding

became such a huge issue with the three women under the same roof that Dad had to step in.

"Look," he told his sisters as they were hanging up clothes to dry in the noonday sun. "I know how you feel about the situation, but Father is lonely. He needs someone as he is getting older. When the two of you get married, who will tend to him?"

One sister was not in the mood for such diplomacy. "She is not a nice person," she fumed. "She doesn't help around here at all and she yells at everybody like we are her personal servants!"

Dad had eyes and could see that it was not a happy marriage. But it was not his place to confront his father about his poor choice in a wife. Instead, he turned to his sisters and reassured them that he would soon find them husbands and they would no longer have to put up with their new stepmother.

Dad had grown up under the wing of his father who owned and operated his own photography company. Grandfather was known to create magic with a paintbrush and Dad spent many a day watching him create humble masterpieces and selling them. The painting thing was really out of Dad's league, but he naturally took to the photography aspect of the business. Dad has many memories of being in the darkroom watching as his father took photos through the development process. As with the blank canvas in his father's paintings, Dad would watch the blank photo paper become works of art … art which was not out of his league, and which quickly became second nature to Dad.

Since the moment he dropped his bags at the door upon his return from war, Dad was ready to start his new life. He was compelled to take the torch from his father as my grandfather was getting along in years and losing business to his brother. In fact, my grandfather's business had officially gone under, leaving Dad to branch out on his own. Hell would freeze over before Dad would join his uncle, so he started working out of his apartment.

By the time Dad took over my grandfather's business, he had moved out of the house and into a small place in a nearby city. He was also working a "bread-and-butter" job to make rent and other basic expenses as some kind of delivery man. But being the *Undercover Sailkot Indian Artist*, he would often sneak up to the mountains and take pictures of nature in his spare time. He kept a camera in a leather bag that he slung over his shoulder wherever he went.

As Dad tells it, it was a very grass-roots effort. He put together a make-shift darkroom in his small bathroom by blocking out the light and using a portable basin in the bathtub for developing photographs. He pinned the photos to wire hangers hung over the shower curtain rod.

Then it happened, a conversation with one of his old army friends he ran into while in town.

"Hey, how's it going?"

"Good. What have you been up to?"

"Oh, I've been working. Nowadays I'm doing the photography thing." Dad reached into his sack and pulled out a photo he had taken recently.

"Oh, nice." His friend held the photo, impressed, "I know some people who would like this."

And that's how it started. One sale led to another and Dad's name became well-known for his photos. At the time, the army demographic was an untapped market. And Dad, being the shrewd entrepreneur from a family of entrepreneurs, quickly realized that he was sitting on a potential goldmine. His connections gave him first dibs on the inside track. For instance, there were needs for certain supplies like canteens or paper. Other times they needed pins for weapon-making. And that was just the tip of the iceberg. There was a whole world of supply and demand for things the average person would never think of - like bolts, knobs, and even shoelaces. Dad quickly became the man to see for more than just photographs. Now he became the man to see for all army supplies. It wasn't long before his business expanded to many other creative, intriguing projects as well. He would get contacted to take professional photographs of political leaders and other wealthy, important people.

My father had always been the independent thinker, the free spirit who followed his heart. As he was building his business, he and Mom had been "dating" on and off, taking things casual and slow. In this world, they were from different social castes. In America or Europe, castes can be loosely compared to what are called *social classes*. People from different castes were thought to have different destinies so they weren't supposed to date and have families together.

Knowing this and the likelihood Mom's parents wouldn't accept someone from his caste, Dad made a bold move: he used his charm to get to know his intended in-laws. He played it low-key and casual in the beginning with him and Mom being just friends. Many times he went over to hang out with the family, playing chess or cards with Mom's father. Despite being from the "other side of the tracks," it wasn't long before they came to know him - and to love him, too.

Mom was very strong, confident and independent. Her motto was that a relationship is based on trust, faith and confidence in self. She came from parents who thought differently than the ideals of a patriarchal society and she and her sisters were always encouraged to pursue their own goals and ambitions. With her father's support, Mom attended the university and when she met my father she was busy working on her degree to become an occupational therapist.

Now this book is supposed to be about me, so let's fast forward.

Three years passed and Mom was finally ready to be married. It was love, and the two of them decided to just do it. Eloping in India in the 1970s wasn't exactly two crazy kids running off to Vegas. In reality my parents *sort of* eloped, going down to city hall to be married by the court judge. Mom's cousin was there and Dad had his brothers present as witnesses. After the nuptials were over, they called my grandparents from a pay phone and told them the news. Progressive or not, this was not a very comfortable moment for anyone involved. Her parents didn't like it, but Dad, being irresistible, won them over again - this time for good. These days if Mom shows up to India without him, the family wants to know all about how he's doing.

As mentioned, Dad was the head of the house and it was his job to find suitable mates for his brothers and sisters. He was an awesome matchmaker. His first success story started with his brother. He introduced him to a woman in school studying medicine. She relocated to the United States to intern and had gotten her green card. That was how it all began. The citizenship of his brother's new bride opened the door for that brother to come over. Then, one by one, two of his brothers and one of his sisters moved. She relocated to Canada and two of his brothers moved to the east coast of the United States, while another brother relocated to Holland. With almost the whole family now in North America, they began nudging Dad to make the move, too. He suddenly had a decision to make. His life was prosperous. He had a family of his own now. He had everything he could want - and he was just getting started. But it was a communal culture. And families stuck together ...

The choice was difficult. If he moved it would become a sink or swim situation. Being in the United States, a place on the other side of the world, he would suddenly find himself without an occupation, a reputation, or a community. It would be as if he had been completely stripped of his identity. No longer would he be the esteemed artist and businessman, he would have to start from scratch.

This was indeed another moment at the well, but he wasn't that 15 year-old kid anymore. Should he travel to a new world to be close to family or stay where he was already established? Once again, Dad rolled up his sleeves and squared his shoulders. It was that time in life where change was knocking at the door and he was going to have to choose between moving forward and staying behind.

Even though Dad has no regrets, he often wonders if it was the best choice.

Whenever I ask him what his first impression of America was, he always laughs heartily and his response is simple: *it was the land of opportunity, the Promised Land, the Holy Grail* … a reputation leaving little room for personal impressions or opinions, I suppose.

By the time he and Mom immigrated to the States in 1979, my sister was two and I was a seed unborn. Driven to succeed and provide a good life for us, Dad took up work at a local pizza shop. He was a photographer by trade, so manual labor was quite an adjustment. It all came to an end one fateful day when he cut his finger slicing pizzas and had to go to the hospital. It was pretty extreme. And to make matters worse, he was broke. It seems that if you don't have money, you get the worst medical treatment possible. A foreigner without insurance walks into the ER and they page the intern. But a band-aid wasn't going to fix this. The cut was so deep that he had to have surgery.

Whatever the surgeons did made a bad cut turn into a damaged nerve. Many times Mom has told me the tale of Dad's drooping, nerve-less hand still holding his newborn son, cradling him close. That was my dad. He never gave up, gave in or let anything stop him. I suppose that same spirit is what enabled me to survive the road ahead.

2

Life Before the Microchip

<u>*The Microchip*</u>: *my personal reference for my mental illness, a way of describing the dysfunction that occurs in my brain, otherwise known as paranoid schizophrenia.*

As I was growing up, my father was a little like Dr. Jekyll and Mr. Hyde. He had two sides: there was my *dad* and then there was *The Man*. *Dad* was his bright, beaming side - the playful *Undercover Sailkot Indian Artist*. Then there was *The Man*. *The Man* was his dark shadow - the perfectionist who constantly applied pressure to do more and be more . *Dad*, the artist, did what he wanted; *The Man* did what he had to do.

I did everything I could to please *The Man*. When I was in fifth grade I started working at his store in Lebanon, Pennsylvania. He owned quite a few businesses over the years and, at the time, he had a beer distribution warehouse. It wasn't pretty - just a huge dusty stockroom with piles of beer cases and a cement floor. You didn't come in for ambiance, just for beer and some snacks. At the warehouse people couldn't buy alcohol by the bottle, only by the box. While I swept the floors and cleaned up in the back, many a stranger would come in to pay *The Man* so they could drown their sorrows by the caseload.

As a kid, everything was an adventure to me. I'd run up and down the aisles of stacked beer cases counting each one, playing whatever mental games I could invent to make it more interesting. *The Man* would yell at me to stop. I think what he wanted to be an apprenticeship, like he had with his father, turned more into him babysitting me while running the store. It seemed neither of us could understand why the other was behaving the way they did.

The Man and I were in the beginnings of a life-long culture clash. There he was, looking at me playing and having fun wondering what was wrong with me and why I was so irresponsible. Meanwhile, I looked at him wondering why he was so angry at me all the time, except, of course, when he was *Dad.* On those days, if he was in an exceptionally good mood, he'd let me bring my dog to work. Boy, those were fun times. I'd have somebody to play with and it was entertaining seeing my dog in a different environment. She would have fun sniffing stuff and exploring the warehouse. I'd try to stay in the back so when the bell hanging over the door jingled, I wouldn't get into trouble. That was the unspoken rule: when a customer came in, I had to be quiet. And if my dog saw someone unfamiliar enter the store, she would start barking. So I would try to keep her in the back, too.

Concerning the culture clash, I had mixed feelings when observing *Dad.* I admired him more than anyone. He was very business-minded, sharp and highly intelligent. On some level, he was my childhood bully, my nemesis and my best friend. *Dad* was my entire world - a gifted soul who lost his own dreams for the good ol' American dream.

He wasn't a bad person - just an amazing human being with a very illuminated side and a searing dark shadow as well. Even at seven years old I recognized this on some level and every day became a strategy of me trying to please him enough to keep *The Man* away. There were, of course, lighter moments such as the family parties where *Dad* would dance and sing. He'd serenade my mother. He loved to sing and he loved my mom. She was the love of his life.

Shubi S.

Perhaps he was a child like me once upon a time - sensitive and eager for his father's love. But in his homeland, affection between men was not allowed. Life was hard and there were difficult lessons to be learned - lessons which couldn't be taught through hugs and kisses. In his world, a boy became a man through hardship and by figuring things out on his own. Guidance and teaching were luxuries.

For me, born in Reading and raised in Lancaster, Pennsylvania, guidance and instruction were more like necessities. My soul was gentle and my heart was big. Living in a small town nestled in the rolling hills of the Pennsylvania countryside, it was a comfortable American life, with not much else to do but work at the store and play with my dog.

But let's go back to where we left off at the end of the first chapter. We moved around quite a bit. After injuring his hand at the pizza shop, *Dad* was disabled and needed to find less physically demanding work, so he began selling insurance door-to-door. Being the charismatic guy that he was, what started out as a gig with an unsure future (particularly for a foreigner with a heavy Indian accent) turned into a big success.

As the story goes, Dad eventually saved up enough money to buy his first house in Reading. His brother's family stayed with us while my uncle was getting on his feet. And although *Dad* had been doing well at the insurance thing, finances were still tight all around.

But in my world, everything was happy. The communal environment was very stabilizing to me. What was there to complain about? I had two boy cousins to play with all day and the whole family was together. My cousin Chinku (his real name) and his older brother Manu (his real name, too) were, and still are today, my best friends. The three of us spent a lot of time running and playing. We did our share of getting into trouble, too. Later in life, as things went downhill, these same cousins would become part of the support system that would help me in my salvation, but we'll get to that later in the story.

As I grew older, although I was myself American, I recognized the difference in the cultural values and norms between my family and the other kids. Asian/Indian culture is more rigid and structured - a more communal kind of living in contrast to the autonomy of American society. The goal is not to be on your own at 18. In Indian culture the family *is* your community. You share everything, everyone knows what everyone else is doing and they know what time it's being done. There is not nearly as much independence. This has its advantages and disadvantages. Most people see the stereotypical Indian doctor and wonder how they scored high enough on their SAT or MCAT tests. It's the drive to succeed that is so embedded inside the culture. My mom is that way, my sister is that way, even I have it to some degree.

My first exposure to this cultural difference was with my dad. I realized that although we were related, we spoke two different languages. *Dad* spoke broken English with a heavy accent and I, on the other hand, spoke English with no accent. I understood the language he and Mom spoke at home, but for some reason when they called me in Hindi I would always answer in English.

My second realization came when we moved to Delaware. *Dad* had saved up enough money to buy his first property. This was the big one. Eavesdropping on my parents talking in the small cramped house we shared with my uncle and his family in Reading, I picked up on the significance of how this venture was going to give *Dad* the money he needed to afford us a better life.

The next thing I knew, we were in the car on our way to Delaware. I didn't want to move away from my cousins, but Dad promised we would only be there until the business, a deli, got off the ground. I wasn't sure what getting off of the ground meant, but when we pulled up in front of the tattered building, I had a pretty good idea. From the looks of things, this wasn't a weekend project. It was definitely going to be long enough for me to miss Chinku and Manu and be very lonely for a while.

Shubi S.

My parents enrolled me and my sister in Catholic school. It was the beginning of fourth grade and, for a ten-year-old Hindu boy, quite unnerving.

Catholic School was different than the public school I had attended back home. For starters, because of the high tuition, I was introduced to a whole new demographic of kids from more privileged families. On the flip side, public school was more of a melting pot with kids from different cultural and socio-economic backgrounds. There weren't many, but in public school there were at least a few Indian kids here and there. I had attended public school from kindergarten to third grade and the kids in my class all grew up together. By the time I left, the insults had already been traded-in and everybody was used to everybody.

In Delaware, I walked up the mounting series of brick steps to a stoic building with statues of people, none of whom looked like me or my family, postured outside. The sign above the front entrance read "Saint Edmund's." I wasn't sure who Edmund was, but he must have been important to have a school named after him. And when the principal walked me into the classroom to join the other kids for homeroom, I became a brown spec in a sea of pearly white.

At lunchtime, the teacher, who did not permit talking during class, left us to socialize among ourselves for half an hour as we sat at our desks eating whatever our parents shoved into our lunchboxes that morning. I was reaching into my brown paper bag when one of the kids asked me, "What's your name?"

I didn't have an "American" name like Bob or Tim, so when I told him, he sneered at me.

"What kind of name is *that*?"

Shubi was a Hindu name, but I was too insecure and afraid to say anything else in my own defense. Immediately, the sound of snickering rippled through the room, making me want to put the paper bag over my head and run home.

After that, a day didn't go by without hearing, "Hey, Indian boy," with kids swatting their hands repeatedly to their mouths making the "whoo-hoo-hoo" sound. It didn't matter to them that I wasn't Native American "Indian." These same kids made sure to invent new limericks for me on a weekly basis, too.

On most days, once the yellow school bus (another prime place for kiddie torture) dropped me off to go home, I'd decide to act as if nothing happened. I knew it was a stressful time for my parents, who were busy with the headaches of repairing and flipping the property they'd bought, so I'd do my best to keep my misery quiet. When Mom would ask how school was, I'd lie and tell her it was fine. Happy to hear it, she'd fix me something to eat and I'd drown my sorrows in food, pretending that I didn't have to do it all over again the next day.

I was soon to face another culture clash when the time came for me to participate in St. Edmund's religious ceremonies. It was already an adjustment wearing the same outfit every day - clothes I would never wear under normal circumstances. Uniforms aside, it was mandatory that all students attend church meetings once a week. Every Wednesday, in the spirit of going on a field trip, they'd walk us over to the church, which was semi-attached to the school building, for service.

I didn't mind. The church was a scary, yet beautiful place. The ceilings seemed endless and I admired the colorfully stained windows. Although it was always cold - in a dead, still kind of way, with the musky combination of incense and old mothballs thick in the air – I thought it was a magnificent building. It was fascinating seeing the strange men in their long flowing white robes, sparkling jewelry and fancy hats, and the pale women in long black dresses wearing what looked like black and white bonnets on their heads.

Shubi S.

Everything was fine until one of the women in black came and stood at the center of the aisle to usher us into line formation. There I was, seated in one of the last rows, swinging my feet hard enough to touch the songbook holder on the back of the next pew when she and I made eye contact. My ears heard her telling me to get up, but my butt was frozen to my seat. The kids were going up to the altar to receive something called "communion." I watched nervously as my classmates bent before the old white guy in the long robe with their mouths open while he inserted what looked like round crackers onto their tongues. Whatever this "communion" was, it seemed scary, so I refused to move. My teacher came over, upset. I tried to explain to her that I could get into trouble at home by doing something outside of my culture. Instead, I earned myself a reputation for being rebellious. After the "communion incident" the faculty called my folks to come in for the first of what would be many parent-teacher meetings.

By the time *Dad* finished rebuilding and then selling the store, fourth grade was over and it was back to Lancaster County where Dad had bought the beer warehouse mentioned earlier. He and Mom were making better money, so they placed me in *Country Day School*, one of the most competitive institutions in the country.

Country Day is an elementary school and high school all rolled into one. The high school is on one side and Kindergarten through 8th grade are on the other side. This was a whole new world for me. In terms of socio-economics, it blew Saint Edmund's right out of the water.

Lancaster County had, and still has, a lot of "old money" and high priced citizens. It wasn't unusual for my classmate's parents to be doctors, lawyers, real estate tycoons or politicians. With my family, my parents were business owners who were doing well financially, but they weren't quite wealthy enough to "keep up with the Joneses." Nonetheless, Lancaster County is also Quaker country and personal financial wealth isn't often flaunted.

Murder and Misunderstanding

Being new, I caught some slack when I first got there, but eventually my ethnic background began to not matter so much as the other kids got to know me. I even made a best friend – "Noland" – an Orthodox Jewish kid. We were like two peas in a pod. "Noland's" father was a radiologist who had his own medical practice in Lebanon, Pennsylvania - not too far from *The Man's* beer warehouse. I didn't really play with too many kids outside of my family, but "Noland" was one of the exceptions. I would ride my bike over to his house and we would play together. Over the years, "Noland's" family took me under their wings. His mother was one of the kindest people I've ever known and his father was one of the smartest. I was really close with "Noland's" siblings too. I became an honorary member of their family.

In school there were a couple of us who flocked together at lunchtime. There was me, "Noland", a Russian kid named "Dustin", "Shawn" and this kid named "Paul". "Paul" was tall, awkward, lanky and really intelligent. He was the kind of smart that was so beyond everyone else it made him strange. He was into Star Trek and some other weird stuff. Dude was really out there, but he was cool.

Then there was "Shawn". "Shawn" got A's on everything without even studying. We went on bike rides and he ate at my family's house sometimes. Years later he still remembers me inviting him to one of my family events where, as he says, "there was good, spicy food and old, wild women dancing to past midnight." (I never would have imagined that this guy would one day have his own internet business and end up designing the cover for my book).

Another guy I hung with was "Mike". "Mike" was a nice kid who had cystic fibrosis. The disease left him really underdeveloped and skinny. Even though he was a teenager, he didn't look any older than eight. I admired his commitment to getting good grades despite the fact that his life expectancy was only a few years. I didn't keep in contact with him after graduation, and when he died I felt really bad about it.

I spent most of my weekends hanging out with my cousins. Our family was a tight community. We fought like anyone else, but we were always there for one another. Throughout my life's experiences with schizophrenia, they were the ones who saved me, kept me from falling off the cliff and passing the point of no return. They covered my sins and provided for my material needs when most parents, sisters or cousins would have wiped their hands clean. A support system is really the X-factor with mental illness. I wouldn't be around to write this book without mine.

But let's get back to the family for now. Typically, it was me, Chinku and Manu who hung out together when we weren't in school. Our fathers were brothers and my cousins were my best friends. I could call them up anytime and ask what they were up to and they would pop over or I would go to their house. We watched movies and did normal "kid stuff" like playing hide and go seek and kickball. Like most other kids we LOVED ice cream and went to the ice cream parlor any chance we got. In the summers, we made it a point to find an ice cream truck or go to Dairy Queen even if there were two quarts of the stuff sitting back home in the freezer.

A favorite indoor pastime was playing video games. We had competitions that rivaled the Olympic ceremonies. I unfortunately sucked at Nintendo and usually had to take the heat from Manu as he beat me in testosterone-filled triumph. We made it a habit that no matter whose house we were at, we'd find a big bed and all of us would pile on top and chill out - gossiping, joking around, listening to music and reminiscing.

We also loved to explore the outdoors. Our neighborhood had a lot of trees and we loved building our own forts in the woods. We went to the arcade, enjoyed water-gun fights, and just went for walks around the neighborhood.

Murder and Misunderstanding

We weren't a delinquent bunch like the kids who smoked, drank and bullied other kids, but we could be mischievous at times. In one incident Manu and I filled up the water drain in my backyard with rocks and anything else we could find, causing the water to back up inside the house. We sure got in trouble for that one. Chinku got yelled at, too, even though he wasn't actively involved, which is why he remembers it so well. Injustices always seem to be some of the strongest childhood memories.

Ironically, Chinku was the most mischievous out of all my cousins. The adults in our family called him "terror" because he would stuff his mouth with chocolate chip cookies until his cheeks were about to explode and then run around pinching us so he could show us the mush inside his mouth. He did things like that because he was younger and knew he could get away with more. One time he was trying to look at something outside the window and literally stepped all over my face to get to the windowsill. It wasn't funny back then, but it became a hilarious memory for us as grown-ups. He always wanted to do what his big brother and I were doing. I remember he got green with envy when we were allowed to ride the lawnmower for the first time. He couldn't because he was too small, but we were practicing for our driver's test.

My favorite memories were the big sleepovers with all the cousins together at one house. There were eight of us total. We loved to change into our pajamas, get some snacks and watch scary movies. One night, we were watching "Bloody Mary", a horror flick about an evil spirit who materialized whenever someone said her name aloud several times in a row. We challenged each other to lock ourselves in the bathroom and call her name out three times. We were young and silly, and got easily scared after just one "Bloody Mary" escaped our lips from behind the closed door. Then, when whoever was behind the door, alone, started to panic and tried to come out, several cousins would lean on the door, locking the terrified individual inside. Of course, whoever was stuck in there was screaming for their life. Another game, probably the best game of all, was called "Light as a Feather". One of us laid on the floor while the rest of us repeated the words "Light as a Feather" over and over again as we tried to lift them up using only one or two fingers each. I had a lot of fun back in those days. I suppose these are normal childhood games, but, regardless, life was good.

My high school years were lived out at the beer distribution warehouse *Dad* owned and operated. I'd be at *Country Day* from eight in the morning to three in the afternoon, then at the store with *Dad* until dinner. I found myself living in two different worlds. The first half of the day was spent just like everyone else - a kid trying to get good grades and throwing spitballs at my friends from across the room. At night I was working in the store, trying to fill my dad's shoes. And those were big shoes to fill. I wanted so much to succeed because I admired him, loved him ... and feared him. Deep down, I knew *Dad* had good intentions. He came from a village where they were hard-working, good people who wanted their kids to do really well. In his own way, he wanted to make me into a man. But I wasn't in a village, I was in America. The road to being a man held different pitfalls and challenges for me. It would be years before my father and I would come to realize this.

As I got older, I started working in the warehouse moving boxes. When customers came in *Dad* would run the register. Sometimes, a customer would want cold beer and I would go in the freezer at the back of the store to send the chilled case to the front on the conveyor belt. I'd also arrange the cases neatly and try to keep track of the inventory. For instance, if someone bought a case of beer, I would replace the newly sold item in the storefront.

During this time in my life, I can't say I was isolated by my peers. Nor would I say I was an outcast. In our class there were only 50 of us, and we made the journey from fifth grade all the way to high school graduation together. I liked and got along with all of them. However, I did feel the pressure of attending school during the day and working in the store in the evening. Adding to this stress, I was also rather insecure and unsure of myself.

Outside of school, some of my classmates did drink and smoke both cigarettes and weed, but that never bothered me. I figured it was their choice. What was frustrating at times was that I had to go to the store after school. As a result, I didn't really get to do much outside of school besides work.

High school was also the time I was trying to figure out who I was and where I fit in. Trapped between my inheritance of *Dad's* legacy and what I wanted to do with my own life, school was my outlet to dabble in new things that someone from my culture would never have had the chance to experience otherwise.

Basketball is a good example. Somehow I thought that joining the team would be a great idea. In American society, as a guy, the pressure to play sports is ever-present. Athletics is the way boys express themselves and how many carve out their identity. Those who excel are given the respect and admiration we all want - especially from the girls.

The basketball team seemed non-threatening. Country Day was a small private school, so making it onto the varsity team wasn't really a problem. There was nothing to worry about, except for the fact that I sucked at basketball. There were a lot of "Urkel" moments for me. I put on many a real live comedy show as a discombobulated Indian kid trying to dribble and run at the same time. When I'd get out there on the court, my hand-eye coordination was so bad that even the white guys laughed and shook their heads. One day, during practice, I remember I was making my way up the floor when someone passed the ball to me and it hit me straight in the face, breaking my glasses and making them fly off in dramatic fashion. I suspect that I was supposed to put my hands up to catch the pass (maybe this is why there's no Indians in the NBA). The only reason I stayed was because my mother really wanted me to keep at it. But, finally, after months of torture, I couldn't take it anymore. I broke down, told Mom I couldn't do it anymore and retired my jersey. Luckily, I discovered varsity tennis. Now there was something I was good at.

In retrospect, I have to admit, during that time, around 11th grade, I'd become quite a good-looking young man. I'd been hitting the weight room daily, developing myself a nice physique. And with a thick head of silky black hair and a somewhat fashionable brand-name wardrobe, I don't mind saying I was attractive. Of course, I was still insecure and shy with the ladies, but did manage to get asked to the prom by one or two girls anyway. Generally, I had good relationships with people. I was the guy who was nice to everybody. I wasn't the captain of the football team or anything, but I wasn't a social outcast, either. Still, I found myself trying to grab a hold of my purpose in life.

Every morning when I'd wake up to get ready for school, there would be butterflies in my stomach and my pulse would be was racing. I always dismissed it. It was nothing big - I was a teenager. Eventhough, walking into school gave me a reason for anxiety every day. Between pop quizzes, SATs, sports, peer pressure, and cute girls that I was too shy to talk to, being anxious was nothing outstanding. But I knew. There was something more to this. I think *The Microchip* became activated the day my English teacher assigned Eli Weisel's, *Night.* Having a Jewish best friend and being close to his family - on top of being in a school with a high Jewish population - really connected my emotions to the graphic detail of events that took place in the Jewish concentration camps. A tidal wave of empathy swept over me and I was distraught for days.

I decided to keep it to myself and hide my inner turmoil, continuing my usual routine with friends as if nothing was wrong. Inside of me swirled a vortex of intense thoughts and feelings that made me afraid of being alone with myself, much less sharing it with anyone else. If they

Murder and Misunderstanding

knew, I kept wondering, what would they think of me? Not that I had time to dwell on my new emotional turmoil. During the day, school was demanding. And afternoons at the store were even more demanding. *The Man* yelled obscenities at me non-stop:

I was dumb. Incompetent. Lazy.

My father had a way of calling my name that sent ice needles up and down my spine, piercing my soul with sheer terror. He thought the criticism would make me stronger. Maybe it would motivate me to excel, to push harder. But it didn't. It became like slave labor. It felt that way anyway. Maybe it was more like indentured servitude, because at some point I was supposed to be the land owner. I didn't know how *that* was going to happen - especially when I was working hard toward a destiny that wasn't mine. I was neglecting my own dreams for my father's - the same way the *Undercover Sialkot Indian Artist* neglected his dreams for America's manifest destiny years ago.

Truthfully, there wasn't any time to "find myself". By the time junior year of high school rolled around, I was extremely stressed. Studying for the PSAT and SAT college entrance exams had me frazzled. I was an average student, with grades in the B and C range. Test-taking wasn't exactly my forte and on top of it all I was feeling completely lost. Every other conversation in the halls or at lunch period was about college - where you wanted to go, how the application process was going, what the guidance counselor said, how high you scored on the SAT… the one question that never came up was *if* you were going to college to begin with. That option didn't ever seem to be on the table.

I knew my parents wanted me to go to college. After all, my sister and I were the first generation of working immigrants in this country. College would be the milestone of success that my parents could look upon to signify that all their hard work and sacrifice had been worth it. My sister (who is two years older than me) did really well in school and was already in her sophomore year at a college in New York, setting the precedent for me to follow.

School wasn't my thing, though. I was an entrepreneur at heart, but I didn't know what I was really passionate about doing. The expectation was for me to work with my dad, but at the same time get my education. Taking this into consideration, as well as the fact that all of my parents' friends' kids, my cousins, my sister, and every Indian kid I knew both near and far all went to college. I sucked it up and began filling out college applications and sending them out like a good Indian boy was supposed to. Looking back, I see that my mom and dad thought I would go to school, get my degree, pick up some new skills and bring all that back to work with the family.

Waiting to hear back from schools was nerve-wracking. With an uncertain future, I passed the time working for *The Man*, and hanging out with my cousins and two friends from my public school days, "Jesse" and "Freddy". "Jesse", "Freddy" and I resembled the *Three Musketeers* when we were all together, though that was seldom. "Jesse" was an Indian kid, like me - except he was extremely mischievous and was always getting me into trouble. "Freddy" was the adventurous one. I'd met him in nursery school. He was the all American, blonde hair, blue eyes, apple-pie prototype. He played quarterback on his high school football team and was the gentle giant of the group. His parents were the "cool" parents - modern day hippies with the split-level ranch home, two cars in the garage, and a very laid-back parenting style.

In fact, I had my first drinking experience with "Freddy". One weekend I stayed at his house camping out in his backyard. With the tent, flashlights, portable TV and sleeping bags, we were having a blast when, all of a sudden he said, "Hey, wanna drink?"

"Drink?"

"Yeah." He told me to wait while he went inside. A few minutes later he peeled back the tent flap smuggling several bottles of alcohol from his parent's "free-for-all" liquor cabinet.

"Cool," was all I could say. It was wrong, but really exciting. I was finally getting a taste of the life that my classmates who didn't have to work for their father's had. Pouring the drinks into our thermos cups, the two of us proceeded to get tipsy and laugh uncontrollably into the night.

One of the few times the three of us were all together, my parents had gone out of town. There I was, the house all to myself, a teenager's dream. I called up my buds and they both came over.

It wasn't long before "Jesse" had an idea: Girls. He knew some girls that would come over and he began making calls. At the time, my parents had a Jacuzzi, but the heater was broken. To make it work, we boiled pots of water and poured them into the tub.

"I thought this was a 'hot'-tub?" one of the girls asked, shivering.

"Yeah, can't you turn on the heat?" another girl said.

There we were, us in our trunks and our female guests in their bikinis sitting in the freezing Jacuzzi, miserable. "Jesse" tried to suggest that alcohol would cure the problem, but I knew they were uncomfortable. And if they were uncomfortable they weren't going to want to do anything else. They ended up getting dressed and going home. I was pretty sure this wasn't how Saturday night without the parents was supposed to turn out.

One day, when I got home, the mail was sitting on the table. "You got a letter from one of the schools," Mom yelled from the kitchen. Hands trembling, it seemed like it took an hour to open the thin envelope, which looked to be the size of a rejection letter (everyone knew what thin envelopes meant when hearing back from colleges). When I finally got the envelope open and unfolded the thin, creased stationary, the word 'CONGRATULATIONS!' jumped out at me in bold black print across the first line.

"Mom I did it," I screamed, running into the kitchen, excited out of my mind. Really, I was relieved. I hadn't been motivated to apply to many schools and my grade point average didn't exactly give me much incentive. But I didn't care. My fear of failure had been alleviated - at least for the moment. I was accepted to Pace University in Manhattan and was on my way to New York that fall.

3

School Daze

Manhattan was crowded, noisy and exhilarating. My dorm looked like a regular city apartment building. In New York, the rooms were small compared to what I was used to, but I really didn't mind. I was finally out on my own - no parents, no beer warehouse and no more of *The Man* looking over my shoulder. My sister was going to a school nearby and my best friend "Noland" was at NYU, so I had plenty of company there.

That first week was amazing. There was the euphoria of being away at sleep-a-way camp along with the nervous anticipation of being on your own for the very first time. Another thing that stood out was the independence factor. College kids seemed a lot less cliquish than high schoolers with a broader base of people to interact with. Socially I felt like a kid in a candy store.

On the flip side, registration at the school's administration building wasn't so exciting. All the paperwork was a drag. I couldn't wait to get it over with so I could get back to my dorm, unpack, and look over my class schedule for the semester. While in line at the financial aid office, I observed the other kids also waiting to hear their fate. All kinds of people were there -Black, White, Asian, Latino. They were from different parts of the country and even the world. I really felt as if I was a part of something bigger and greater than myself.

That first week was when I met "Amy". She was very sweet and pretty. "Amy" was "Cantonese" - at least that was what she called herself. "Cantonese, not mandarin speaking," she would say. It was hard to forget, because she called herself Cantonese all the time and corrected anyone who said otherwise.

"Amy" was a breath of fresh air in the big city - especially for a guy who had a mother that cooked and washed his clothes for him his whole life. I was a mess. It was hard for me to figure out my eating plan. We lived in a co-ed dorm and her room was a few floors below mine. In the evening she would stop by my room. I'd be sitting there snacking on junk food surrounded by fliers for pizza or Chinese food, not having eaten for the entire day. She would be shocked.

"Didn't you eat?" she'd ask. The cafeterias were located in the student center and in between classes I'd sometimes stop and grab a sandwich or something. But the dorm didn't have a cafeteria - just snack machines and kitchen areas on every other floor.

"C'mon, let's go eat, Momma's Boy," she'd tease me. "You are NOT going to eat Cheeetos every day!" And so she cooked for me - things like instant rice, ramen noodles and other "quickie" foods meant for the college life. While it certainly wasn't Mom's, it was good, and the closest thing I could get to my mom's delicious home cooking.

The same scenario happened with my clothes. One look at the tall pile of dirty laundry amassing beside my bed and she'd had all that she could handle. I didn't know how to wash clothes. My mother had always done it and I had no clue as to what I needed in order to get the job done. "Amy" knew all about those things, so she told me to put my clothes in a laundry sack, bring them downstairs to the washroom and she would do them.

"Amy" and I hung out a lot those first few weeks. We got very close very fast. I began thinking it was love - at least what I knew to be love back then. I even brought her home to meet my parents during winter break. It was uncomfortable having her stay in my room. We'd be making out with my mother right down the hall. It didn't help that she was Cantonese. My parents liked her - I mean they were very open-minded Hindu people, but, at the end of the day, an Indian girl would have suited them better.

Despite my happiness with "Amy", something was not right inside. I had left *The Man* back in Lancaster, but he was still there with me. His voice resonated loudly in my head, echoing inside of my skull the steady sound of failure and doom.

I was still stupid ... lazy ... incompetent.

So when "Amy" came to my room during spring semester to tell me she was pregnant, I didn't know what to say or how to act. Pregnancy forced me to think about the big picture of life. I was still a child, trying to please *The Man*, with no identity of my own and no peace of mind. Being a father was too far outside my point of reference.

It all seemed so surreal. When I looked at my girlfriend, she didn't look pregnant. Maybe it would have hit home if she had been seven or eight months along and I could have seen her round belly poking out at me. But I didn't ask for this. The reality of creating a life while not even wanting to was hard to digest.

I kept thinking, *if we have the baby, will we finish school? How will this affect our career goals? Wait a minute - we didn't have any career goals yet. At least I didn't. What happens when we become parents and we finally figure out what the hell we want to become? By then, will it be too late?*

Unfortunately, these important concerns were reflected on in isolation -"Amy" on her side and me on mine - individually and alone. The separation led to us growing apart and dealing with the situation in our own ways. In retrospect, I should have been man enough to step up to the plate and give "Amy" the security and support she needed. I should have been strong enough to hold her in my arms and say "Hey, no matter what happens, we'll make it - the three of us."

But I didn't ... I couldn't ... I wouldn't.

After several days ... or maybe it was weeks of ambiguity, "Amy" found a clinic and got an abortion. When she told me, her voice sounded dead and numb. She looked exhausted and pale, like she had been pulling two weeks of all-nighters. I didn't know what to say. We both just sat there in my room on my bed, uncomfortably silent. Deep down, we knew things between us would never be the same. My lack of support made her resentful towards me, which ultimately ended our relationship.

To cope, I decided to self-medicate by drinking the pain away. Losing both "Amy" and my unborn child was tough to handle emotionally. That sinking feeling of failure began growing inside of me again. *The Man* was there in my head:

You know why this happened?

Because ... you're lazy ... stupid ... incompetent.

Classes were hard to pay attention to with all the negative thoughts swimming between my ears. It felt like I was trapped inside a Peanuts cartoon, with my professors going "wah, wah, waaahhhh!" I wanted to study finance and since students were not allowed to officially declare a major until sophomore year, I was taking pre-requisite courses that semester. Bored and uninterested in my general education classes, I began drinking regularly. Much of my time was spent going to bars with

Murder and Misunderstanding

"Noland" (who was in New York studying theater). I also hung out with my sister and her friends a lot. At 18, it felt cool stepping into a bar with an entourage of older women. Hanging with an older crowd also allowed me to get drinks without being carded. Most bars and clubs didn't seem interested in the drinking age anyway -not with all the money flowing in from the college crowd.

As far as I was concerned, no one thought anything was abnormal. No one pulled me aside and asked if I was okay because I seemed a little excessive in my behaviors. Good or bad, how unusual is it for a college kid to drink himself under the table, go from girl to girl and struggle in school? I wasn't sleeping around, but I was drinking and, when I managed to hook up with an Indian girl between drinking binges, it went unmentioned. It didn't last long, anyway. She was nice, but in my heart she was only there to distract me from my troubles.

Because of my newly acquired bad-boy partying habits, I was constantly oversleeping and missing class. All night parties and bar-hopping occupied most of my free time, leaving little room to study for exams. Some people were masterful at test-taking. They could be wasted from Thursday to Sunday, miss half the semester being hung-over and still score well on exams. I was not one of those people. My grade point average sunk to below a 2.0.

By fall of sophomore year I had lost my zest for the future. While I was by this time officially a finance major, and I really enjoyed what I was learning, my classes were getting more demanding and work-intensive. And with the last semester's grades in the toilet, I was now on academic probation. If my GPA wasn't above a 2.0 by December, it was bye-bye college career.

All of the dramatic turns and twists made the future look uncertain. Whether I would graduate and what I would do after graduation was nebulous at best. Every time the anxiety grew inside me, I would drown the reality of the situation in alcohol and marijuana. I only experimented with weed a little in high school, but my college roommate was constantly getting high and I was desperate for anything that would put a smile on my face and kill the pain - even if it was for only a few hours. It was a confusing time. I found myself caught between a rock and a hard place. I wasn't motivated enough to stay in school, but I didn't want to go home, either.

By the time Thanksgiving vacation rolled around, I had dropped out of several classes. It was after the deadline to withdraw, leaving me owing the money for the courses. Sensing impending doom, I called home and Mom answered. She put *The Man* on the phone.

"How's school going?" His voice was heavily accented and came in sharply enunciated bursts.

"I'm not sure," I said flatly.

"What do you mean 'not sure'? Talk to me! Tell me what is happening!"

I surrendered and told him the news of my most recent failure. *The Man* wasn't about to put up money for me to flounder around in New York, especially since I wasn't sure of what I wanted to do anyway. And as usual, he had perfect timing. He'd just purchased a new business down in Philadelphia and needed help running it. He suggested I come back home to work for him. And that's exactly what I did.

4

Troubled Waters

At the age of 19, while my classmates were in spring semester of sophomore year, I was home working for *The Man*. His latest business venture was an Italian deli in southwest Philly. It was quite a different experience from my days at the beer distribution warehouse. This time I was working in the kitchen making the food. The deli was in one of the inner city neighborhoods and the customers coming in were rowdy and belligerent.

For a small-town country boy, life in the "hood" made me feel like a fish out of water. Flipping burgers, making hoagies and frying up cheese steaks in a small kitchen without any windows began to take its toll. I was still fumbling around and I could feel *The Man*'s disapproval. He seemed to always be looking over my shoulder as I worked the hot grill and served customers for hours on end. On days that he had to be elsewhere he'd call to check up on things.

It was a tough transition. I tried to get the orders perfect, just the way the customers asked, but the fries were always too greasy or there was too much cheese on the cheese steak. Customers complained, they shouted. One time a guy opened his sandwich and tossed it at my head over the counter to demonstrate how shitty a job I had done. I was a Hindu. What did I know about making Italian hoagies, cheese steaks, fries and burgers?

The worst part of the day was when I had to count the money and close out the register. It was a cash-only business and I wasn't the best at counting money, or record-keeping. I would misplace the receipts and, at times, the sheets wouldn't balance. When *The Man* would look over the books, he'd be furious. So the next day, I'd try harder.

The pace of the rat wheel began picking up speed. I was working so hard to please him, but *The Man* couldn't be pleased. He wanted more - more profit, more success, more of everything that I couldn't give him. I found myself on the edge of the proverbial cliff, about to plunge into madness.

Meanwhile, *The Man* was on a roll. It wasn't long before he bought another property - a liquor store in New Jersey. Pretty quickly, I found myself working at both places, commuting daily between Philly and Jersey - two hours each way. Sometimes I would just sleep at the liquor store because I was so exhausted and too tired to drive back.

That's when things really started to go downhill.

Mom began getting sick. She suffered from dizzy spells that left her in bed for hours, and sometimes days, on end. Since Mom was the backbone of the house, life became very uncertain. The doctor bills were piling up faster than *The Man* could pay them - at least as far as he was concerned. There was never enough money in his savings for him to feel relaxed. He came down on himself hard and then on me, since my mother was no longer able to help him run the businesses. He kept telling me that I had to work harder, longer, better in order to help support my mother during this time. It was either I work or she work. And I couldn't have her suffer any more than she already was.

It was another visit to the well. For the second time in his life, *Dad* was facing the most important woman in his life being taken away too suddenly and too soon. But this time he wasn't alone. We were both standing there and he expected me to take on the same responsibilities he once did. In his world, a boy became a man by saddling up and carrying the load. So that's what I chose to do ...

... After I came back from summer vacation.

An uncle of mine had relocated from India to Holland. Ever since I was nine or ten, my parents would send me overseas to stay with him for a little while. He was a cool guy. He owned his own business - an Indian restaurant in The Hague, right next door to the Dutch embassy.

Every year, once I was old enough, my uncle would have me work as a waiter in his restaurant. I had little confidence in myself, but was a decent waiter. I was horrible at washing dishes though. At any rate, things would be cool for a couple of days, but then my uncle would become *The Man*. He'd start asking me questions about what I was going to do with my life. Once the interrogation began, I knew my vacation was over and it was time to go home.

Of course, back home, it was the same dynamic. Mom was the nurturer. She would talk and talk and talk. On the flip side, *The Man* was hard-core. He'd give me a car, a store, whatever was necessary at the time and tell me to go out there and be somebody.

I suppose this makes sense, considering he'd had a harsh introduction to the world. *The Man* didn't come from a lot of wealth. His dad was a photographer who owned his own studio and raised six sons on his own. Out of all his siblings, *Dad* was the brightest star. He was the most successful and the most generous. They all admired (and still admire) and loved him. And, because he feels partially responsible, he's very proud of each of them and what they have become. It's been this way my whole life and when I was 19, I didn't feel the same pride he held for his siblings, nor do I believe he understood why I couldn't be more like them.

On a lighter note, summers were and are fun. My family loves to throw parties. Growing up, *Dad* was - and still remains - a great dancer. In fact, many members of my family are. Our philosophy - there are never enough reasons to celebrate. We all love to dance. Family events are a huge thing for us. A lot of these get-togethers are thrown by my uncle who lives nearby. He loves to party. The festivities usually involve a table full of great food, good music, and *Dad* singing songs to my mother - the woman of his dreams, his only fear and weakness.

A vivid memory of mine is my uncle, *the partier*, coming to visit one night and sitting in the basement talking about *Dad* for hours. He went on and on about *Dad* - how he'd gotten his brothers married, put money in their pockets, and was the most respected member of our family. Many were the selfless acts my father performed for his siblings. My uncle said that was where I'd gotten my big heart from. Despite my issues with *The Man*, this fact has always been very obvious and true.

That night, I also realized that I was respected in my family. People saw the illuminated, beaming light of *Dad* inside of me. That's why, when things started falling apart, it was so difficult to see myself spiraling downward into madness. Every day when I rolled out of bed and went to the mirror to brush my teeth, I had to decide that, although *The Genetic Microchip* was buzzing inside my head, I would just handle it the way *Dad* would. No self pity and hard work. After all, I thought, looking at my thin gaunt face, I was a survivor just like he was.

Back at the fast-food joint in Philly, the constant bombardment of tension became toxic. Weight was falling off of me with every drop of sweat as I was worked long hours in highly stressful conditions. I could literally feel the pressure, which quickly evolved into a physical pain in my body. My nose would bleed regularly and my neck and head would play a painful duet. The aching was so intense I would get up in the middle of the night and take hot showers to relax my muscles. As the steamy water dripped down my face, I would close my eyes and have visions of me saving the world. When I opened them, my pupils would no longer be focused.

Long days and sleepless nights began to take their toll. I became a zombie. I couldn't even speak coherently anymore. Mom would ask me if I wanted something to eat and all I could muster was a grunt or a mumble instead of a simple "yes" or "no".

Meanwhile *The Man* was pushing himself hard in his work and not paying enough attention to his diet and his stress levels. Mom made him visit the doctor and he came home with a pill bag and a diagnosis for type 2 diabetes - along with heart problems. In the small Hindu village where he came from, there were no heart problems and debilitating weaknesses. A man pushed on and that's what he did. After the many trials and adventures he'd endured throughout his life, a little thing like high blood sugar wasn't going to stop him. So *The Man* soldiered on - which meant I had to soldier on, too.

A few months later he sold the deli, so now it was just me and the Jersey liquor store. *The Man,* meanwhile, was busy starting up other businesses, so he couldn't be there every day looking over my shoulder, showering me with criticism. One of his purchases at this time was some townhouses in South Jersey. Since they weren't too far from the Jersey liquor store, I asked *The Man* if I could stay in one while I worked at the store. He agreed. I packed up my duffel bag, threw it into my trunk and headed to Jersey. The apartment was in a bad neighborhood - the kind of neighborhood where police sirens were ongoing. I turned off the car engine and looked across the street at my new home.

What a dump.

I crossed my fingers and hoped that the car would still be there in the morning.

Shubi S.

The walk up the creaky stairs leading to my third floor apartment was quite interesting. Rap music was vibrating through the walls on the ground floor. On the second floor I heard a couple fighting with each other (it sounded like the guy was cheating on his girlfriend with her cousin). The third floor was quiet and still. I used the key I had gotten out of *The Man's* drawer and went inside.

Luckily, the last tenant had left the light bulbs in. When I flipped the switch, it made sense why the rent was so cheap. I found myself standing in a small, square living room, with a "half-stove" and a refrigerator against one wall, supposedly the kitchen area. The entrance to a tiny bathroom opened up on the other wall and the bedroom door was next to it. No chairs, tables, or television to watch. I did have my radio that I had brought from home. Maybe I would get a little TV later. There was one good thing, I told myself: I was on my own. Sighing heavily, I dropped my sleeping bag on the paint-streaked wooden floor and pulled out my cell phone to order some pizza. The car was still there the next morning when I left for work.

I was relieved to not have to travel back and forth every day if I didn't want to. Now, I was working mainly by myself with *The Man* keeping tabs on me by phone. I clinched my teeth every time he would call because, although he meant well, *The Man* was not good at communication. He was unhappy from a distance.

Eventually, he hired a manager for the store and, as I wasn't needed as much, I moved back to Lancaster.

The days and nights turned into one long, continuous loop. While I was working fewer hours, there was still a lot of getting home late. Mom would have a plate put aside for me and, after wolfing it down, I'd get ready for bed to do it all again the next day. What I would later come to know as *The Microchip* was wearing me down and my threshold for stress was becoming lower and lower.

Murder and Misunderstanding

In 1999, when I was 20, one night turned into more than enough. I was on edge and *The Man* was home when I got there. He wasn't in a very good mood. Neither was I. We got into a huge debate.

I went into my room, slammed the door and slid down onto the floor. Trembling from anger, I grabbed my cell phone and called "Noland", trying not to cry, but I broke down. "Noland" didn't hesitate. He put me on three-way with his father, the *Jewish Radiologist*, who was very compassionate and eager to get me out of there. That day, his parents were on their way to visit him in New York, so they swung by the house to pick me up.

I was scared when the car pulled up outside. Only the walls were supposed to talk. I wondered if I dishonored the family by going outside for help. But enough was enough. *The Man* had gone too far this time with his bullying. Fueled by intense emotions, I began throwing clothes into a duffel bag. He thought I was incompetent and useless without him. It seemed that every time I took a step forward toward manhood by working harder, he would knock me ten steps back into humiliation. And I was determined to prove him wrong by going out on my own without his help.

"Noland's" mom stayed in the car while *The Radiologist* came inside to get me. *The Man* wasn't home. He had stormed out. As far as he was concerned, with my erratic behavior and seeming ungratefulness for the opportunities he provided me over the years, I could get out and stay out. My mother didn't agree, but she didn't have control over *The Man's* actions, his words or his temperament. She asked *The Radiologist* if she could get him something to eat and he politely declined. Worried, she kissed me goodbye and told me to call her when I got there to let her know I arrived safely.

While standing there in the hallway watching *The Radiologist* ease mom's mind about where I would be staying, I wanted to break down and cry again, but resisted the wave of strong emotions washing over me. Instead, I threw the bag over my shoulder and walked out to the car and got in. *The Radiologist* was a humble man. He made a lot of money, but still kept a low profile. I appreciated this part of him as I slid into the backseat of his aging black Ford Explorer SUV. His wife was glad to see me and was very concerned about how I was doing. Her eyes were soft and kind as they peered into my soul.

We pulled off and it wasn't long before we were on the highway headed to my best friend, "Noland's", apartment in New York City. As the car cruised down the freeway, *The Radiologist* and his wife chatted and listened to the radio while I rolled down the window and leaned my head against the sill. The breeze rushed over my face and made me feel alive again as memories of vacations with "Noland's" family flooded my mind. I would show *The Man* I didn't need him.

5

On My Own

"Noland" was staying on the upper east side of Manhattan in a two bedroom apartment with another high school friend of ours, "Julie". The surroundings were relaxed - not just because of the nice place he lived in, but because of the family as well. They were loving and gentle - an elixir to the harsh words of *The Man* assaulting me at work and at home. I walked around the apartment looking in all the rooms, amazed by the tranquil quietness inside the walls. "Julie" was very savvy with interior decorating and I admired the pretty curtains rustling softly in the breeze that flowed through the huge brownstone windows.

"Noland" was just like his parents - gentle and kind-hearted. I slept on the couch which he insisted on preparing for me. The only thing missing was the mint under my pillow. Feeling awkward, I told him that he didn't have to go out of his way to make me feel at home, but he would hear nothing of it. While in town, *The Radiologist* and his wife stayed at a hotel and took us out to eat and spent time with us. But, after a few days, they left for home in Pennsylvania. They always made sure to treat me like one of the family. It was nice. It was also a chance for me to pretend I was someone else with a different reality for a while.

As much as I was moved by my best friend and his family's generosity, I knew I had to get my ass out there to find a job. So the next day I began sifting through the classifieds, which was not an easy task.

As I read qualifications for job after job, my insecurities came back to haunt me. I had worked for *The Man* all my life. This was unfamiliar territory. I'd never had to make a resume or go on an interview before.

"Noland" lent me his suits to go on interviews and let me use his fax machine to send resumes out to businesses. The days were flying by and the end of the month was fast approaching. "Noland" and "Julie" were cool about it, but I couldn't let myself get too comfortable. When they were showered and leaving out the door for class and their part-time jobs, I made sure I was up, dressed and holding a newspaper, opened to the classifieds in my hands. Just as things were beginning to look hopeless, I came across an ad for a financial company in Hoboken, New Jersey. It said "no experience necessary" so I was definitely intrigued – not the least because I had been a finance major back at Pace. This seemed to be the type of job I would be interested in doing if I had actually graduated.

I spoke to a guy on the phone who told me to come to their training seminar. They hired me on the spot. When I got back to the apartment *The Radiologist* was there. He was in town checking up on "Noland" again. I remember sitting on the living room couch with a company pamphlet in my hand, proud to show it to him.

I did it! I wanted to yell as loud as my lungs would allow me. *I got a job on my own ... without The Man!*

"Noland" and *The Radiologist* were really happy for me. They knew the obstacles I'd had to overcome for this one victory. They also knew I was into finance back in college. Many times we would have debates while driving places in the car about what a hedge fund was, or if small caps versus large caps worked better over time. I thought large caps were better and "Noland" took small caps. Then *The Radiologist* would chime in and set us both straight. Those were fun times.

Murder and Misunderstanding

At my new job, victory soon turned to sorrow. The place reminded me of the movie *Boiler Room*. I found myself working in a cramped space full of desks, phones, computers and slick guys in suits and ties, all hungry for the next sale. The game was selling options on foreign currency. It was my job to pitch these scrappy investments to people by cold-calling them and convincing them that these investments were the next big thing. But being a bad liar, I failed miserably and it wasn't long before I got canned.

For "Noland" surviving wasn't an issue. New York was simply a training ground for him to be on his own. His parents were financially sound and he was just testing the waters of his own independence. When his and "Julie's" lease ended we all decided to rent a huge house with one other guy in Williamsburg, Brooklyn. The rent would be lower for each of us and we could stay together. Now the pressure was on for me to make my share of the rent, so it was time to get the classifieds out and start job-hunting again.

I landed an interview at a small, but lucrative human resources company on Park Avenue in the upper east side of Manhattan. The office had two ends to it - a high end where they placed people in first tier jobs and the low end where they put people in the $15 an hour bracket. When I walked into the office the owner's wife was there and we talked for a few minutes. I could tell she liked my personality and before I left I had a new job. I was hired to be her personal assistant - answer the phones, file paperwork. For the next six months I filed stuff away, cold-called people, and set up the computers for clients to take skill aptitude tests for job placement. It was a small office with about seven employees.

The owner of the company was "Harry" – an older guy in his fifties who wore glasses and towered over me with his six-foot-plus frame. He was a well-respected, polished and very wealthy black man. He was also a brilliant businessman who had contracts with different companies throughout the tri-state area, the banks being one of them. The bank contracts earned him 30 percent for his referrals. I was daunted by his confidence and strong presence whenever he walked into the room and, just like I did with *The Man*, I tried hard to get his approval.

"Harry" was really nice - cheap, but nice. I didn't get paid much, but I could see that he was testing me, trying to figure out if I was going to fit into his organization on a long-term basis. Because of my insecurities I had a tendency to overcompensate which made me seem cocky. Part of this cockiness had me in a "I'm going to be a millionaire myself" phase. I acted as if I had split personalities. One minute I was arrogant and trying to impress him, the next I was being nice and trying to make him like me. Then, I was back to being resistant again. His strength and resolve reminded me of *The Man* - a resolve that was unappeasable in my eyes. And just like with *The Man* I had trouble defining who I really was and focused more on trying to be who I thought he wanted me to be.

"Harry" saw my pain and tried to reach out to me. He invited me into his office to talk many times. Instead of being myself, I'd find myself trying to dazzle him with my skills by throwing around textbook phrases from my finance college textbooks. One day, I told him that I could reduce his business cycle - which was a lie. Another time I tried to pitch him my t-shirt idea. His logo would be on it and everything. He just looked at me and chuckled. I didn't know a thing about any of that stuff.

The highlight of coming to work was "Harry's" niece "Sara". She was tall, slender and beautiful - with smooth, dark skin and long curly braids that swung freely with each turn of her head. I had a huge crush on her. "Sara" wasn't just a pretty face. She was really sweet and had strong values. I admired that a lot. She was my motivation for coming to work every day.

And I needed some motivation, too. Life in New York wasn't the same care-free experience I'd had during my college days. My salary wasn't measuring up to my Big Apple expenses. With a bi-weekly, take-home pay of $600, I was barely making ends meet after rent, travel, food and other things I needed at the time. My only big-ticket purchase was a bed I ordered from 1-800-Mattress. As I sat on the floor of my room on my new bed wearing one of "Noland's" suits and eating a poor man's feast of bread and oil, I thought about calling *The Man* again. But my pride wouldn't let me. I was just going to have to deal. And I didn't want to ask "Noland" and his family for anything more than they had already done for me.

Back at the office, I put up a front as if everything was fine. I should've told "Harry" about my struggles because I think he would have understood and raised my pay some. If I'd told him about my family situation I think he would have been more understanding. If he only knew that I didn't have a great home to go to. He even stopped at my desk once and commented,

"You know, I don't think your father treated you that well."

He made that assessment on his own, despite my constant bragging about my perfect rich family. "Harry" didn't buy into my act. My parents were doing great for themselves to be sure, but I was over-inflating it for show, hoping to compensate for my weaknesses.

Then, one day, *The Man* called me. Or maybe I was the one who called him. I don't know why. Probably because "Harry" had let me go and I was heartbroken. As his wife's personal assistant, she and I had become very good friends. The small office had become my family. But, as I said earlier, my behavior was inconsistent and I suppose that wasn't good for the business. At any rate, I was broke, without a job and had rent to pay. No matter how much I wanted to show him I could succeed on my own, I just couldn't sever the ties completely.

The Man had news for me. He'd just purchased another store and had a new offer: I would own the store this time around. Since what I had been doing involved certain skills like telemarketing, *The Man* insisted I return home to help increase sales and get things moving. *Dad,* the lighter side of him, was beaming and his loving arms reached out to pull me back in once again. I thought that by taking the store, I could kill two birds with one stone - I'd be financially secure and have my freedom at the same time. So I returned home.

6

The Conspiracy Begins

The new purchase was another liquor store, this time in New Holland, Pennsylvania. And true to his word, *The Man* came through on his promise, giving me complete ownership, with my name on the papers and everything. Now I was doing it by myself for the very first time, a real one-man show. At first, things felt great. I was making really good money and my head was clear. Having my own store was exciting. But, it wasn't long before the hamster wheel began spinning again.

Realize, while I was under a lot of pressure in New York, the change in environment had made me feel safer. Sure, riding the subway was a lot different than the Jersey turnpike, but, for some reason, even on a train packed with strangers, the bad feelings left me alone. Somehow, in the big crowds, I had felt protected. I didn't have to be alone with my thoughts.

Now, back at home, it was as if the Jersey store responsibilities kicked into overdrive. I thought it was bad having *The Man* looking over my shoulder, but now *I* was the one who had to be the problem-solver and the progenitor of anything that needed to be done. It was more long days and longer nights, leading me right back to where I was before I'd left for New York.

The store was inside a small, suburban strip mall, putting me in the line of traffic from shoppers and passers-by. The front of the store had all clear windows, too, giving the public a first-class view of me hustling and bustling inside.

In the beginning, *The Microchip* didn't just turn on and stay on, it would act up and fizzle out and then act up again - especially when I was stressed. I remember one afternoon feeling uneasy. I was moving boxes around when my back began to tingle. It was if someone's eyes were on me. Suddenly the sound of people talking loudly pierced through the air, bursting the silence like a pin to a balloon. Startled, I jerked my head around to see a group of teenagers walking by the store. The front door was propped open for customers and to let the warm summer air in, so I rushed over and kicked the brick out of the way and pushed it shut. It was glass, too, still leaving me exposed - which didn't feel too comforting. My next project consisted of me stacking beer and wine-cooler cases in front of the windows to give me some kind of fortress. I tried to fight it, but the sharp pangs of paranoia were jabbing at my insides on an "on-again-off again" basis.

Since there was no one to talk to, I would be inside my head a lot. When the thoughts became too much and were spilling out, I began talking silently to myself. And the more I got into myself, the more the people around me looked suspicious. That, and the stress of being a store owner really exacerbated my paranoia.

The first time it happened, I had worked a long day at the store. It was dark out when I sludged over to my car for the drive home. As usual, traffic on the highway was jammed. I looked once at the glaring lights in my rearview mirror … then again. And then a third time. With each sharp blare of an impatient car horn, electric sparks shot through the inside my head in multiple directions.

"C'mon!" someone behind me shouted out of their window. The lane was moving and I wasn't paying attention. Startled, I hit the accelerator. I couldn't stop staring in my rearview mirror, though.

Murder and Misunderstanding

The lane suddenly stopped again. I hit the brakes, making my bag roll off the front seat. Among the glowing red brake lights, people were talking on their cell phones, drinking coffee and blasting music. I noticed that the car directly behind me was a Volkswagen - a German made car. The guy had a suit and tie and a pair of shades on. He laid his hand on the top of the steering wheel and looked directly at me.

Oh shit.

I ducked down so my eyes wouldn't see him in the mirror. Then I rolled down the window and checked him out in the driver's side reflector.

His head slightly turned to lock eyes with me again. Now he was watching me watching him.

A break in traffic opened up and we were off and cruising at the usual speed limit again. Increasing momentum, I switched lanes two or three times - weaving in and out of the other cars. I just had to see. Both hands gripping the wheel, I checked the rearview mirror once more.

The guy was still behind me!

I sped up, panicking. Something was wrong. I began flipping through my mental rolodex in an attempt to figure out what the hell was going on.

Why was I being tailed? Maybe it was my brown skin. Being raised in a strong Jewish community, I had visions of the Holocaust and of the shady dealings of car companies using concentration camp victims as slaves in factories making their cars. I remembered Eli Weisel's, *Night*, from my high school days. The visual made the stress build up inside my chest as I continued to weave in and out of the fast lane. I checked the rearview mirror again. The Volkswagen was gone.

Shubi S.

The next night I was in my car and again, I was being followed. Behind me off to the right was another Volkswagen. The windows were dark, so I couldn't see inside, but I knew it was them. After some more thought, I realized that the rabbit hole ran deeper than I could have ever imagined. These people following me were hired by somebody and these "somebodies" wanted to keep an eye on me for sure. I suspected it was some kind of conspiracy.

The next night on my way home was the same scenario. I spotted the VW logo in my mirror again. Trying not to be too obvious, I gradually eased my foot down on the accelerator while plotting how to lose them. As I exceeded the flow of traffic, it seemed that the other car also increased speed to keep pace.

With them right on my tail, there was no way I could go straight home. I scanned my mind frantically, looking for a quick solution. The sign for the next exit popped up and, as if on cue, I sharply twisted the steering wheel, sliding across the middle lane to the exit ramp, almost crashing into the car in the inside lane along the way. At the end of the ramp was a stoplight, which was red. Afraid to look in my mirror, I slammed my foot down on the accelerator and made a sharp right. No cars were coming from the opposite direction, so I kept going until I hit the third stop sign. I made a left and then another left. By the time I felt safe enough to pull over I was on a dark, tree-lined street with rows of nice houses and manicured lawns. Coming to a stop in front of one of the houses, I turned off the engine and unbuckled my seatbelt. The sweat was rolling down my forehead and my heart was beating in my chest like an acoustic drum. I was exhausted both physically and mentally. I had no idea where I was, but it didn't matter. I was just relieved to be safe.

There was still one order of business: I had to figure out why they were tailing me.

You're a threat.

I checked the car radio and it was turned off. No one was on the street or in my rearview mirror.

"Why?" I asked myself.

Because you are representing all black and brown indigenous peoples in America against the White power structure. You're taking them to task.

"What does that mean?" I responded, resting my head against the steering wheel.

It means you're the front man for the class-action lawsuit. You're demanding reparations for Blacks.

"Well, what am I supposed to do now?"

Keep your eyes open. Take nothing for granted. They are watching you and you must stay ten steps ahead of them until this case gets won!

"Who's 'they?' Who are these people following me?"

"They" are the powers that be, The Microchip informed me. *"They" remain behind the curtain, but they send out their representatives to do their bidding. Watch everybody. Trust no one.*

Confused, anxious, but more resolved, I checked behind me again and stuck the key in the ignition. It was time to go home.

Meanwhile, my parents were under the impression that I was going to go back to finish college. After work, I'd get home tired and the dinner table would be a place where I was under the spotlight. In between bites, *The Man* wanted to know what my long term goals were. I was frustrated because I couldn't even enjoy my food. Wasn't owning a business enough?

"You checked out any schools yet?" *The Man* would ask.

Shubi S.

Hell no, I thought.

"Uh ... I've been busy, but I'm going to look into it."

These conversations left my head hurting and gave me a feeling of uneasiness that was sinking in deeper and deeper. After a few nights of interrogation, I'd get snappy. *The Man* and I constantly got into arguments about what I was supposed to be doing with my life. I hadn't applied to any of the local schools he had suggested and I wasn't running the store the way he had hoped. He remained persistent in asking me about how my store was doing and if I was meeting profit margins.

All the questions made me suspicious. After dinner one night I was laying in bed with both eyes wide open, staring at the ceiling.

He's one of them.

"Huh?"

Your father. He's one of them.

I sat up, rubbing my face in an attempt to shake it off.

He's too nosy ... asking too many questions. Watch him.

Distressed, I yanked the covers over my head and rolled over to hibernate.

But before I fell asleep that night, I made a decision. If I wanted to be safe, I had to cut myself off from *The Man*. He kept asking me questions because he knew something and wanted to find out about the class-action lawsuit. I figured that the process of elimination would be best. Maybe if I stepped away I could tell whether *The Man* was a part of the conspiracy to destroy me or not. It would also help ease the confusion and stress. After all, I had the store in New Holland. I'd run it myself. I didn't need him. I didn't want to admit that he was the one who had given me the store in the first place. I found an apartment in New Holland and cut *The Man* him off - told him not to call, not to come over, and to leave me alone. The commute was definitely faster.

One day, when I pulled into the parking lot of the strip mall, it was scattered with parked cars. Things were pretty quiet - a little too quiet. It didn't feel safe out in the open, so I hustled into the store quickly and closed the door, reluctantly flipping the OPEN sign over for customers to see. As I unlocked the register and got the store ready for patrons, I felt like I was in a fog. It was as if I was in a role in a play, starring the Hindu liquor store owner. It was one o'clock in the afternoon and I knew *The Man* would be cringing at me for not getting there at the crack of dawn to work from sun-up to sun-down. If I wanted to make this business work, I was going to have to be open for as many hours as humanly possible. Yeah, that's what he would have said if he could have seen me that day.

Running a store gave me the opportunity to do some serious naturalistic observation. Things were pretty slow before dark. The liquor crowd didn't kick in until after five - the time when people were getting off work, but didn't want to go home. It wasn't exactly the wine and cheese crowd. Customers would come inside and be extremely ignorant. Mainly white males came in looking for beer, vodka or other hard liquor and they weren't expecting to see my face.

The later it got, the more ignorant they got.

"Hey Habib! Get me a case of Miller Lite."

"Habib! Gimme change for a twenty."

"Hey! Hey! What's your name…Habib? How much is this?"

I hated being called Habib.

Shubi S.

One night, in my apartment, I was sitting on the floor blowing through a bottle of caffeinated soda and listening to the my new hero:

Tupac.

Pac always had something good to say. He was raw, gritty and kept it real. Bopping my head to the music as he rhymed the words to "I Wonder if Heaven's Got a Ghetto," I was in the zone. I loved black people.

You're one of them.

"Yeah?"

They are your brothers.

I listened as I ripped open a bag of chips.

The class action lawsuit. It's for all of you. The American Social Order is out to destroy all oppressed peoples. Stay on your mission.

I sighed. Here we go again.

After that, the dark cloud engulfed me completely. I had a feeling of impending doom. Somebody's eyes were always watching. Something was chasing me. Whenever I left work, I'd have to keep checking the rearview mirror because I was being tailed. I could feel it. The nights were dark and the downtown traffic was thick with cars, glowing red break lights and blaring horns, making it hard to see who it was, but I could feel it.

It was the Germans.

I started thinking that Germans were out to get me. *The Genetic Microchip* was shooting sparks throughout my system, signaling for me once again to pay extra close attention to German cars that were following me as I drove back and forth to work. My memories of reading about the Jewish Holocaust in high school brought new life to my suspicions. I once again thought about the stories of how Jews were forced to work as slaves at German car companies as free labor. That was part of the conspiracy. Germans and their cars couldn't be trusted.

I would find my foot applying more and more pressure to the gas pedal as the feeling intensified, hoping I could outrun them. They were everywhere.

Each time I served a customer, *The Microchip* would tell me they were an undercover agent trying to get to me. When customers were in the store, the chip would send out a signal to let me know what was up. I found myself becoming very aggressive, not just with new customers, but with the regulars, too. I had no choice. With me on public display, I was a prime target for infiltration. Somebody (or sombodies) had an eye on me. I could feel it on my skin, which began to itch, making me very uncomfortable. Then *The Microchip* sent me a message:

You must smoke out the spies.

"What?"

That's right. Smoke 'em out.

I decided to put a sign up in the store that said "cover charge". That way the customers who were out to get me could be weeded out. I could catch anyone trying to get something over on me. In reality, all it did was cause people to become irate with me. But, as far as I was concerned, I already suspected they were secret agents sent in to infiltrate the business, so their anger made me accept the messages *The Genetic Microchip* was signaling to me even more. Why else would they be so upset? If they had nothing to hide, what was the big deal about paying a service fee?

Shubi S.

With the ongoing saga of the cover charge, I quickly gained a reputation for arguing with customers. A guy came in and set his beer case on the counter and I pointed to my hand-made sign, signifying a service payment. The guy looked at me, glanced back at his girlfriend waiting by the door and then looked at me again.

"Are you kidding?"

"No."

I wasn't budging. There was a lot at stake here. He got pissed off and I got even more adamant. He then proceeded to curse me out and storm out of the store. I didn't care. Another guy was attempting to buy beer when I demanded the cover charge again. He refused and I didn't like his vibe. When he slammed the door behind him, it was good riddance.

I underestimated him, though. He and a few other disgruntled customers went to the sheriff's department to complain about the cover charge and my aggressive behavior. After a couple of visits from customers, I became somebody "of interest" to check out. It wasn't long before the door opened and two patrolmen came into the store to give me a warning. Surely they had better things to do than tell me how to run my business. According to them, people were complaining about me and I was being labeled as a "danger" to the public. That little visit confirmed my feeling that I was being watched more than ever.

It wasn't long before they were back and I was being led out in handcuffs. Two hours earlier, I had been in a confrontation with another customer. When he refused to pay the cover charge, I lost it. I screamed at the guy across the counter that he was an agent and that he best get the hell out of my store before I take him to task. His ego wasn't about to let him just walk out on my command, but after a few more moments of heated words, he finally got the picture. He high-tailed it out of there to another store in the strip mall. I ran to the door with a balled fist hoisted

Murder and Misunderstanding

in the air screaming at him never to come back. Apparently I was causing a scene and people walking by were slowing down to observe. Whatever.

It wasn't long after I went back behind the counter to pick up stuff I knocked over in the confrontation before I saw the red siren lights flooding the store. I was furious.

The gangsters wearing blue burst in and wanted to know what was going on. I looked over to the right at the irate customer standing there once again with his arms folded.

"Get the hell out of my store!" I told the blue devils.

We began scuffling. I found myself grunting and twisting, trying to physically resist them at every turn. My sister showed up just in time. She'd been stopping in after work. An accountant at a major firm in Philadelphia, she was helping me out with the books. Knowing *The Man*, he had probably asked her to check up on me and give him behind-the-scenes updates on how bad I was screwing up. She tried to talk to me and get me to calm down, but to no avail. She would never understand. The tears streamed down her face as the officers wrangled me into the backseat of the police car. Not one of my better days, for sure.

This would become the first of a series of hospital stays.

The general hospital downtown was a nightmare. The staff was indifferent and calloused. It didn't help that I was delusional and resisting. They walked past my room only to see me shadow boxing, doing push-ups and acting like Rocky Balboa. I guess I was paranoid, but when you're paranoid, you don't know you're paranoid. If you know you're paranoid then you're not paranoid.

Stuck there in emergency room purgatory, part of me felt like I should have opened up to someone. Each time the doctor or a nurse came into the room, I had a chance to spill the beans. But I couldn't. Not with the lawsuit pending. Worried they would turn against me, I decided to keep my big lawsuit against *the establishment* a secret.

Meanwhile, the hospital decided to keep me for a few days. They moved me upstairs to one of the double occupancy rooms. My new roommate was a cool, thin black guy who was friendly, but looked like he had been through just as hard a time as I had. Compared to me, he was much more mellow and non-confrontational.

My bed was on the side of the curtain next to the window overlooking the hospital parking lot. One day, after the nurse left the room, I stood there, looking outside. Among the neat little squares filled with parked cars was a four door sedan with people wearing business attire inside. They seemed heavily engaged in conversation and kept looking up at the building.

It was the lawyers. It had to be.

I started piecing everything together. The creeps tailing me in their Volkswagens were a team of defense lawyers working for the "powers that be". They knew I was bringing a class action lawsuit against them. I was going to save humanity by legally destroying the white man's sinister plan to oppress the world - especially the people with darker skin.

Another day, I saw a white van parked outside with tinted windows and a hidden camera taping my every move. These attorneys weren't as slick as they thought they were. I was onto them. When I realized I was under surveillance I began screaming and trying to leave. It was a bad feeling being caught in a bear trap while my predators were after me. I was a sitting duck. Every time one of the workers came into my room to give me my medicine, I would slap it out of their hand or refuse to take it. They tied me down to a bed and became angry towards me, calling me names and telling me to shut up. When *Dad* came to visit me, he was shocked to see my mattress on the floor. "What is this? Why are you sleeping on the floor?" he wanted to know. I told him how the staff had gotten pissed and taken away my bed as a way to punish me.

The remainder of my time there consisted of interviews with psychiatrists, psychologists, doctors and social workers - all who thought I was just being a typical punk bad-ass. I wasn't opening up about what was going on inside my head, so my delusions looked to them like rebellion. Without a diagnosis and no reason on paper to keep me, they let me go with a flimsy outpatient discharge plan to follow and a script for a drug I couldn't pronounce.

After I was released, I went back home with my parents. I spent most of my time in the basement. *The Microchip* was in sleep mode and I was mellower than I'd been in a while. Maybe it was the exhaustion of the hospital experience. Or the heavy narcotics they gave me. But the drugs made me suspicious of their motives. I figured the hospital was working with the lawyers to take me out. After all, they did nothing about them sitting outside my window while I was there, except yell at me and tie me down. With me refusing to willingly comply, Mom tried to take on the task of making sure I took my medication. But, every time she handed me the pills, I hid them in my pants or locked myself in the bathroom and flushed them down the toilet. With no sedation, I was gradually backsliding into madness. Now, as I sat there on the couch, a new idea hit me:

How was I going to touch God?

I guess I had always wanted some kind of God-like knowledge, something innate. I was a spiritual person - one who had a lot of time on his hands to meditate. I believed there was a God - he just didn't want to be bothered with stupid things, that's all. God was like *The Man*. He was big and I was small. It was up to me to seek him out and try to understand him. I needed to know what the purpose of my life was. I needed to know the purpose of me going through all of this pain.

The basement had a hole in one of the walls where the old air conditioner used to be. It was at the top near the ceiling and there was a ladder next to it. I climbed into the hole and into the darkness, searching for knowledge. Crossing my legs, I sat in the dampness of that dark space reciting *Yahweh* over and over again in my head. There was a huge conspiracy swirling around me. I was the special chosen one who had a mission. Now I was in a trance.

And *The Genetic Microchip* suddenly grew vocal chords.

No longer was it just thoughts, now there were actual voices bouncing off the walls of my brain. There wasn't much room for anyone else, but, of course, *The Man* wasn't intimidated. He refused to accept anything less than a VIP spot and his real voice had no problem breaking through the internal voices. My vegetative state annoyed him. Maybe he was concerned, but the words "How are you doing today?" came out as "Are you still down here doing nothing? The garbage is piling up. Take it out."

I was slowly making my way to the edge again and, as usual, *The Man* was helping me along.

Parents just don't understand.

7

The House of Cards Crumbles

Over time, my delusions became more and more complex. In the midst of irrationality I would have logical thoughts, though. In a way, these logical thoughts were there to make the delusions make sense - kind of like a string connecting all the delusional thoughts together like beads on a necklace. And after a while I began believing all the fabrications and fanciful scenarios. With this illness, everything that comes into your head is something you feel with every fiber of your being. You believe it is real. You would literally bet your life on it. How could you not believe it when it's all you hear between your ears, day in and day out? My senses were overwhelmed as I imagined the secret conferences where the lawyers were meeting to discuss what to do about me.

With my father, mental illness was a new concept. No one in his village was mentally ill. Men weren't depressed. If you felt bad, you got yourself a drink or you threw yourself into your work. Every day he worked his fingers to the bone while I was camped out on his couch eating my mother's food in his house. As far as *he* was concerned, I had no reason to be "mentally ill" about anything.

With me being out of commission, *The Man* had to step in to run all of the stores. There was just no way I could continue with that much responsibility. He kept pressing me about what I was going to do with my store to the point that I became suspicious of his motives. Reluctantly, I signed over ownership to him and, as usual, he worked his magic. He was a true genius at flipping and selling properties.

Somewhere around 20 years old, my parents couldn't bear to watch me sitting in the basement staring at the walls all day, so they put me on a plane to visit my uncle in the Netherlands. On the plane ride over, I kept looking around at the other passengers, trying to figure out what was really happening. Both logical and delusional thoughts weaved in and out of one another like a quilt, leaving me with a fabric of uncertainty and mistrust.

I was looking out the window at the white fluffy clouds when I heard…

Look around.

I was afraid to. It wasn't so much an audible voice, more like a thought or an eerie sensation. I tried to ignore it by putting on my earplugs and hitting the PLAY button on my iPod. Nothing was loud enough to drown *The Microchip* out.

Look around!

I tried to inhale deeply, but my breath was shallow. I hadn't heard *The Microchip* in a few days and I didn't want to now. I thought about the Twilight Zone episode with the monkey man on the wing of the plane ripping it apart. That was distressing.

"Not here, not now," I answered inside my head. It was as if I was in a dark hole talking to someone on the surface.

Better check to see if you're being tailed.

"Hmmm. Maybe you're right". The lawsuit was still pending. I got out of the hospital and was now free to save humanity from the unscrupulous powers that be. Suddenly I had another dark, eerie feeling:

The conspiracy was international!

Yep. The class action lawsuit involved the United Nations. This thing was bigger than I ever imagined - crossing all borders and cultures. It was them against ALL of us.

Not the most relaxing flight I've ever taken.

At my uncle's house, things were great for the first couple of days. He was my dad's brother and very much like him in certain ways. So it wasn't long until the excitement wore off and we were back to business as usual. Questions of what I was doing with my life kept creeping into our conversations. I kept trying to deflect him to protect myself. And with each inquiry about whether I was going to school, working with the family business again, marriage and other uncomfortable topics, the eerie suspicion began growing inside of me. He could just be overbearing or…

My uncle was in on the conspiracy, too!

I didn't want to face it, but that had to be why he was being so nosy and pounding me with questions. He was working with *The Man* to trap me. Here I was, on the other side of the world and it was my own family who were my biggest deceivers. Deciding that going along with his ideas would bide me time to devise a getaway plan, I kept this new revelation to myself.

In the meantime, I was trying to be normal. While my uncle headed to his restaurant, I stayed home. He told me one morning before he left that I should go into downtown Den Haag - also called *The Hague* - to hang out. He lived in one of the suburbs, but for a young male such as me he thought I would find plenty of fun with the bars, coffee shops and other city life going on down there.

I said sure. Two can play this game. He must have thought I was stupid, like I would walk into the trap that was awaiting me. I knew *The Hague* was the government center of Holland. It was time to head to the restaurant, so he told me he'd see me later and left. I smiled, nodded and as soon as the front door locked shut, I hurried upstairs to shove all my clothes back into my long blue duffel bag. After five days, it was now time to get moving before I had any unexpected visitors.

It wasn't long before I was showered and ready, throwing the track bag over my shoulder to go downtown. The streets in that part of Holland were very clean and uncluttered. I looked around. No unmarked vehicles. I hopped the tram into downtown. Downtown was small with clusters of contemporary buildings and classic architecture. It had a modern but old-world feel to it. Brownstones lined the cobbled, bricked streets under the horizon of towering, "eco-friendly" glass office buildings. I stumbled across an Asian massage parlor on one of the back streets. Desperate for somewhere to sit for a few minutes until I devised some kind of plan, I went in. I also wanted to keep out of the open in case the agents were looking for me.

A cute, Asian girl greeted me. She asked me if I wanted a massage, but my head was pounding and I wasn't in the mood. She insisted I take some of her herbal tea. Immediately she went and boiled the tea and brought me a steaming cup to drink. I was skeptical, but the girl kept saying "*dis is reely reely goowed.*" And so I drank. But the pounding in my head remained the same. And there stood the girl, smiling at me with a "so, did it work?" expression on her face. I smiled back and nodded to be polite. Satisfied, she took the cup and disappeared through the doorway's dangling beads. I grabbed my bag and was out through the door before she came back.

Murder and Misunderstanding

Sipping the warm tea didn't help, but it did give me time to think about things. I didn't feel safe going to where my uncle suggested and I didn't trust him. Not only that, but who knew what would be waiting for me when I got back to his house? I pictured him at work pulling a phone number out of his pocket, dialing feverishly and saying in a low voice:

"He's here."

No way. I caught the next tram to the airport.

I booked a flight to Indonesia. It was a hassle, since I had to convert my American traveler's checks to the appropriate currency. But I managed to get it done and was on the next plane. Once again, being in such an enclosed space for all those hours was frightening. I was sneaking out of Holland to go to Indonesia, the land of freedom. If I played it cool, I told myself, I could slip under the radar and everything would be okay.

My first "thesis" about how to handle the lawsuit was to act normal, so when they falsely arrested me and threw me in the mental hospital I would have a case against them. Now, as I sat there on the plane, the "thesis" was evolving. If anything bad happened, I could claim permanent damages from being harassed by the lawyers and have a rock-solid case. The idea sounded good at the time.

When I got off of the plane, I was yelling and pumping my fist in the air. It was the black civil rights movement and I was standing up against injustice. My pulse was racing and I was free from my uncle - the traitor who was working with my father to take me down. He didn't even know I was gone ... black power!

There are a lot of people in Indonesia. We landed in the capital - Jakarta - a booming commercial metropolis of more than ten million residents. Mostly brown faces flooded out of the terminals as if a dam had been breached and the waters were rushing everywhere. I was leading the charge - a revolutionary happy to be in the land of milk and honey. The streams of people in motion were reminiscent of the million man civil rights march in Washington D.C. I joined right in, pumping my fist in the air. Black power!

The Indonesian airport was amazing. It was huge with many things going on. You had the panhandlers and the people doing shadow puppets. Other people were selling oils and miscellaneous stuff, all begging for your dime. I slung my trusty blue bag over my shoulder and made my way through the crowds toward the exit. I had no clue where I was going. All I knew was that if I put one foot in front of the other, I'd find what I was looking for.

To the left and right of me there were people holding signs, telling me to come to their hotel. This was Indonesian billboard advertising, live and in color. My only reference for such things was when people, such as a limo driver, would stand holding a sign that said *Mr. Smith* so he knew his ride was there. I assumed that's what it must be for me, too. That's it - the hotels had sent ambassadors to pick me up! Cool.

I chose the sign that said "Sahid Jaiya". It was a huge place that was dirt cheap. The hotel had everything - a restaurant, a mosque, a swimming pool - all this crap in the same building. I made instant friends with the concierges, one of whom was a single mother with a baby daughter. I spent my afternoons taking them to the park and out to eat. The girl was pretty young, maybe in her early twenties like me, and was really nice. Like a huge portion of the Indonesian population, she was from Bali and wanted me to go there with her. Maybe she liked me and wanted me to meet her family, but I was pre-occupied with other things. I had a mission to fulfill.

My nights were wild. And on one particular night, while in my underwear, standing in a pile of used food cartons and empty bottles and scratching myself, I heard rapping on my hotel door. I opened the door,

Murder and Misunderstanding

disheveled and half-awake, to see a guy wrapped in a turban and a long draping robe standing there.

In broken English, he introduced himself as "High Priest Imam" (*Imams* were worship leaders in the Muslim religion). He extended his hand and I shook it.

"What is your name?"

I told him.

"Where are you from?"

I told him that, too.

"Ahh! America, huh? I don't like America, though!"

He started preaching to me about Islam. The more he talked, the more paranoid I got.

Looking down at me in my underwear, he asked if I was circumcised.

I said no.

That was the way of God, he said, cleanliness and God. He kept going on and on about me getting circumcised and converting to Islam. I almost started to believe him.

Then I thought about it. At my age, wouldn't circumcision hurt?

"Okay, goodbye!" I eased him out by closing the door in the middle of his circumcision spiel.

"Sunday service at the mosque, 6 AM!" he shouted from the other side of the door.

Extremely dedicated, the high priest came to my room daily, trying to get me to come to services at the hotel Mosque, to circumcise myself and denounce Hinduism. Not that I was really practicing that either, but it *was* how I was raised.

I may have had it under control as far as agents, like the *Imam*, were concerned, but money-wise I was slipping. Two weeks of partying and scandalous living went by and I was out of spending money. The traveler's checks were almost gone. I had to come up with a new plan.

With the little cash I had left, I went back to the airport and booked a flight to Singapore. Originally, I wanted to go to India, but I didn't have a visa. So Singapore it was. I had no clue as to why, but that's where I was headed next.

When I arrived at the airport in Singapore, I was almost out of money, so I decided to stay on the premises. It was an enormous facility with a built-in hotel and all kinds of tourist accommodations - including a bad-ass bar/lounge with all sorts of great things to do. I went to the pool and swam a few laps. It seemed like everyone was looking at me. I felt insecure. What could it be?

I wasn't circumcised! That had to be it. Of course, looking back, it was probably because I was swimming in cotton boxer shorts, which were now soaking wet and clinging to my genitals.

At any rate, feeling like all eyes were on me, I climbed up onto the poolside and gathered the pile of clothes I left when I stripped down. From there I went to relax in the sauna. All the other guys were sitting on the benches in white terry cloth robes, just staring at me.

I became convinced. They were looking at my *thing*. I was an uncircumcised freak!

It had only been a day or two in Singapore, but with this new development, it was time to go. I could already tell Singapore was going to be a rotten vacation. I wanted to get a flight back to America, but was

Murder and Misunderstanding

out of money. I had spent all my remaining cash on the Singapore spa services. I called *The Man*.

"You id-i-ot!" he yelled into the phone in harsh, accented bursts. "God-damn you! What the hell are you doing in Singapore?!" Just thinking about the long-distance phone bill was making his blood pressure rise.

"All I need is five thousand more dollars. You owe it to me!" I snapped back, referring to the money he'd made selling my store, which he had purchased for me in the first place.

"I will order the ticket." he said angrily. "Go to the counter."

I went to the front desk and gave the clerk *The Man's* credit card number to book the next flight home. But, the guy was asking too many questions and wanted too much information, causing my paranoia to kick in. I became belligerent with him.

We were going back and forth across the desk when the head of security - an Indian woman - stepped in. Just in time, too, since the guy was going to stop me from getting on the plane for bad behavior. "He's okay, he's okay," she said to him. "Let me talk to him for a little bit." Reluctantly, he printed out my ticket and I was now in her custody.

The lady said she was from *Rajasthan*, the largest state in the Republic of India. I was psyched to hear it, being that the name meant "the land of kings". She gave me and my blue bag clearance while telling the story of the great warrior class of people in her native land. "Yeah! I'm a warrior!" I started yelling, pumping my fists in the air again. I felt extremely cool. I was a warrior sporting a pair of Oakley sunglasses - a luxury purchase I had made somewhere along the way, but couldn't remember where or when. These glasses had cost about 200 dollars and reminded me of something a race car driver would wear. I was one cool-ass, freedom-fighter. I hopped the next plane home.

But it wasn't a direct flight. I had a layover in Chicago and by the time I exited the plane, my high had worn off and I was in a state of panic. I was back in America, the headquarters of my oppressors. Being on their home turf was extremely unsettling. On top of that O'Hare International Airport was packed and buzzing with travelers, zig-zagging past me in all directions - holding crying children, pulling suitcases behind them, looking frazzled trying to find their terminal.

I found a seat in one of the plastic chairs lined up against the window and observed it all, trying to calm myself down. I had my sunglasses on, so at least I wouldn't be recognized. But there were too many people and too many potential agents walking around. They were waiting for me to get back to the States so they could lock me down under their jurisdiction.

I decided there was no way I was getting on that plane to Philadelphia. In need of resources, I rummaged through my wallet and pants pockets. All I had left were a few Singaporean dollars so I went to the exchange desk to get what money I could for a hotel room. Chicago didn't have an in-house airport hotel like Singapore, so I had to leave the premises to find a place to stay. I grabbed my bag, slung it over my shoulder, and charged out through the front exit. As I emerged from the sliding glass doors, the sidewalks were streaming with people. I was almost blinded by the bright sunlight of the Midwest sun, making my overpriced sunglasses obsolete. Cupping my hand above my eyebrows, I scanned my surroundings for the nearest hotel.

The street in front of the airport had cars and cabbies everywhere. A long line of synchronized yellow cabs waited patiently by the main entrance to get first dibs on potential customers. I had no idea what my next move was. I just kept walking.

"Taxi, taxi!" A dark Mexican man called out to me.

He was the first one to speak, so I figured he was the one. I approached him and, looking him dead in the eye, told him I needed to go to Lancaster, Pennsylvania. The words slid out of my mouth and shocked me as I said them. I figured, forget the hotel. I had to get out of town fast. If I flew in like *The Man* wanted me to, I would probably get ambushed the minute I got off the plane. I still didn't trust him. The lawyers most likely gave him the money to give to me for the ticket in the first place. Why else would he help me in my time of need?

The cab driver spoke broken English, but was able to understand where I wanted to go. He opened the back door of the cab and told me I could get in. I slid into the back seat; he slammed the door shut and disappeared for a few minutes. I guessed he was trying to figure out how to manage such an unusual request. About twenty minutes later, he returned with another Mexican guy and they got in the front. We pulled off and stopped at a gas station to make the first fill-up. I promised I would reimburse them for the cost of the trip when we arrived. The other guy, who didn't appear to speak much English either, pulled out a map and started navigating in Spanish.

The drive from Chicago to Lancaster is about 12 hours, but we had to stop to get food and pump gas along the way, so it took us even longer. With the long trip ahead, the driver gave me a pillow and I slept almost the whole way. This felt like another adventure with me, once again, foiling the plans of my adversaries. The visual of the frustrated agents waiting for me to get off of the plane made me feel much more relaxed. Of course, the meter was running for the entire drive and I kept promising the drivers that my parents would make the trip worth their while when we got to my house.

"Get out of here!" Mom screamed over the fence. The Mexican guys were standing out there demanding their money in broken English, along with a few Spanish phrases I'm sure were curse words. Ten minutes prior, we had pulled up to the front of my parent's house and I told them to wait in the car while I went inside and broke the news to the folks. They were furious. Since I didn't come back out immediately, the cab drivers started leaning on the car horn.

While Mom was outside, *The Man* wanted to know why the hell I hadn't been at the airport the day before and why I didn't answer my cell phone. I'd been avoiding his calls, thinking he was setting me up. Once we heard Mom's usual soft voice blasting angrily from the front yard, we followed her outside. She was in the midst of a heated debate with the two cab drivers. They wanted their money and she refused to give them anything. I think *The Man* would have choked me right then and there except he had two pissed off Mexicans in his driveway screaming and honking the car horn to worry about. They were making a huge ruckus in our otherwise quiet suburban neighborhood. Neighbors were peering out of their windows and looking over the fence to see what the heck was going on.

Mom threatened to call the police. Those seemed to be the magic words to grab their attention. Shouting a few more obscenities, they jumped back in their cab and pulled off. Fortunately for me, the initial brunt of my parents' anger was sidetracked by the drama I brought to their door. It was one of those situations where I had gone so out of bounds, it was almost impossible to wrap their minds around how to react. My sister, however, was a different story. She happened to be home visiting and made sure to lay into me on Mom and Dad's behalf. All told, I'd been away for about one month.

After a few weeks home on the couch - and after everyone cooled down - I went back to the warehouse with *The Man* again, sweeping floors and doing menial tasks. Life was back to normal and "normal" meant one thing: stress and more paranoia. I could feel myself getting fidgety again. My days were spent in front of the TV looking at the turmoil going on in Iraq. It was post 911 and the country had voted George W. Bush in as president. I was really unhappy with how things

Murder and Misunderstanding

were going politically. Every news story or internet news reel seemed to be about the pain that people were in, from mothers protesting the war in front of the state capitol to the funerals for dead soldiers whose bodies were being shipped home in droves.

One day, I'd had all I could take. At the time, Mom had a backup car - a used Lexus that was just sitting in the garage. I grabbed the keys off of the wall hook and hopped in. The roads were pretty clear that day and the sun was shining bright. I was on a new mission:

Ending the war.

My skull was pounding. *The Microchip* embedded inside my head was hooked into the satellites circling planet earth. I believed I possessed an unbelievable power to influence other people's thoughts with my own, kind of like Aquaman on the Super Friends. He would send signals out and get the sea creatures to do anything he wanted. Just like Aquaman, all I had to do was protest the war in my head and magical things would happen.

Washington D.C. was only two hours from Lancaster and I managed to find the White House pretty easily. I parked one or two blocks away on a side street and made my way to the front entrance. As expected, the gates were locked tight, but there was no need to go in anyway. I had telepathic powers.

I situated myself on the ground in front of the gates and settled into a meditation posture, sitting Indian-style on the hard concrete. Then I began to chant - the same way I had chanted in the hole of my basement wall. I could feel the signals radiating out of my head to the satellite dish in the sky and then back down to President Bush in the Oval Office.

As I sat there harnessing my thoughts for Bush to call off the war, I noticed people were giving me signals. Pennsylvania Avenue was alive with passers-by and tourists, many of whom were foreigners wandering around in groups, squinting up into the light, snapping photos. One guy looked down at me in curiosity as he walked by.

It was working.

A woman in a business suit passed me going the other way. She was on her cell phone and didn't notice me at all.

It wasn't working.

I was frustrated at the mixed messages I was getting. I decided to refocus and continue my chanting. *Stop the war,* I said over and over. *Send the troops home...*

"Sir what's your business here?"

"Huh?" I covered my eyes from the sun to see where the stern monotone voice had come from. I don't know how I missed it, but a gang of squad cars and hummers had surrounded me. They were real-life GI Joes parked there. Two or three of them got out of their cars while the others remained in their vehicles with the dark tinted windows. The GIs were wearing some kind of uniforms - a cross between army fatigues and security guard attire.

They ran the plates on the car, which was registered to my mother and called her up. When she answered the phone, the guy introduced himself as a secret service agent and asked her if she had a son named Shubi. I could hear her voice on the other end blaring loudly out of the GI's cell phone receiver, sounding shocked and frightened. She must have told them about my "mental difficulties" because, instead of arresting me, they made me get in the back of their car and drove me over to where I was parked. I stood there as they searched the trunk, under the hood and every nook and cranny of the interior, looking for bombs. Then they sent me on my way with a friendly warning to go straight home.

After the D.C. incident, Dad decided to get me a therapist, a very kind Jewish man. Actually, he was Jewish by name, but religiously he was a Buddhist - not to mention one of those old, had fun at Woodstock, artsy types. Instead of an office with me on a couch, we went to food buffets and hung out all day, talking about my issues. When it came time to pay, I naturally expected him to pick up the tab. I did this for weeks. Finally, one day after the waitress went to get the check, he asked me why I wasn't chipping in. Uninhibited, I told him that I thought he was rich. I was raised in a predominantly Jewish community where everyone had money. He was a psychologist, Jewish, and like "Noland's" father, *The Radiologist*, I assumed he had pretty deep pockets. "I don't have money," he said, amused at my ignorance. After that, I paid my half of the check.

During our therapy sessions, I spent a lot of time talking about my anger with *The Man*. "Doc" was convinced that the only illness I had was ungratefulness. In fact, when he spoke to my Dad (who was paying his fees), he dismissed *The Genetic Microchip* altogether. Dad was disappointed, but *The Man* was relieved. His indifference to my illness was now justified. But *The Microchip* always tells the truth and it would soon prove that its power was severely underestimated.

8

Out to Lunch

I found myself moving closer and closer to the edge again. With my latest misdiagnosis, *The Man* became extremely impatient with my inability to get back to normal. Inside he must have been troubled seeing me like this, but he didn't know how to handle it.

One particular night, when I was about 21, yet another turning point occurred. I was with *The Man* at home when Mom called. Dad picked up the phone and was talking with her for several minutes. Since I was unable to hear her end of the conversation, the truth soon became evident:

The two of them were conspiring against me!

That did it. Now my mother was in on it, too. I expected *The Man* to sell me out, but Mom ... I thought she, out of all people, would be on my side. In my wildest dreams I never imagined she would give in to the establishment. I was edgy to begin with and this new revelation reactivated *The Microchip*, making me unable to hold it in anymore. Now all levels of restraint and marginalized behaviors were gone. I told *The Man* to stop talking behind my back. He snapped at me and we began arguing.

Somewhere in the midst of our exchange I punched him, not hard, but hard enough to cause his sixty-year-old body to hit the floor with a soft thud. Seeing his nose bleeding and feeling guilty and ashamed, *The Microchip* fizzled once again and I offered to take him to the hospital. I asked him if he wanted to go to the emergency room. Remembering the unfortunate trip to the hospital that destroyed his arm many years earlier, he wouldn't go unless hell was freezing over.

"You want to leave the home, don't you?" he said soberly. I must have said yes, because we left in his car, he dropped me off at the bus station and handed me 400 dollars. (I had a suitcase so I must have packed before we left). Looking back, I have to admire *The Man*. I punch him in the face and he gives me 400 dollars rather than getting medical treatment. Maybe that was his way of making amends for the sorrow he caused. The master was setting the indentured servant free with his blessing.

I hopped the next bus to Philly.

I was familiar with certain areas of the city from working at the deli, so I found a small motel in the same neighborhood and rented myself a room by the week. In my mind the question was, how am I going to live here and get a job? But *The Microchip* assured me that it wasn't a problem. After all, I had 400 dollars and a credit card in my name - all courtesy of *The Man*.

That was how they found me. *The Man* got the statement for the credit card in the mail and tracked it to the motel. One night the phone rang. I jumped out of my skin, thinking it was the lawyers.

"W-who is this?" I sneered suspiciously into the receiver.

"It's the front desk. You have a guy down here who says he is your cousin. Does he have permission to come up?"

I squinted my eyes. My mind became a swirl of emotions and suspicions. What if the guy wasn't really my cousin but an agent? How did he find me? *The Man* must have sent him ... but that wasn't okay either. That was it - he and my mother were working with the agents and the attorneys to find me. It figured *The Man* would give me up so easily...

"No. Absolutely DO NOT fucking let him up here!" Exasperated, I slammed down the phone.

Of course I didn't know it at the time, but it was my cousin Nanu. It wasn't long after this event that I found myself out of money and on the sidewalk holding my one suitcase.

There were two options. One, go back home, but I couldn't possibly do that. I was sure *The Man* and the agents were camped out there waiting for me. So, option number two it was. I proceeded to drag my suitcase to the nearest homeless shelter.

As I sat there at the intake desk, I thought about when the New Holland police ushered me out of my store and forced me in the back of their car. It was me versus them. The State put me in that hospital because I was a "minority" who was opening my own business and they wanted to silence me. It was a class-action suit with every minority group against the white power structure of America. I was the savior for the world. They knew if they could interrupt my mission here on earth they had a chance of keeping the status quo in check. What they didn't plan on was me getting sent home from that hospital. And now they were watching my every move.

The first night at the shelter was horrific. The smell of piss stung my nose and made my stomach churn. I was pretty sure that the lawyers were on my tail again. Ever since I saw them parked outside of the hospital, during my unfortunate stay, I knew they were following me. The law suit was still pending, with me raging against the machine.

I remember sitting down to dinner at the shelter one night, the food, gloppy and tasteless. I looked around the long tables at all the distraught, dirty faces just like mine. How did we get here? At one point we were all normal people, working, eating dinner with our family ... living. I didn't feel afraid, just the heaviness of hopelessness, shame and disappointment. No one made eye contact - they just kept their heads in their plates, shoveling down their food.

As the beds were prepared and we stood in line to get pillows and blankets, I realized this wasn't a place where I could let my guard down. Once they called "lights out" and the room got dark, I was nervous again. Maybe I was wrong about being scared, but with my vision compromised by the darkness, any one of these guys could be an agent. I laid there on the hard mattress with my arms wrapped around my suitcase, waiting and watching, trying to ignore the vapors of booze and funk assaulting me from every direction.

My days were now spent trying to shed off the burdensome layers of my existence. One day, I used the travel pass I had bought with my remaining spare change to go to the airport. The seats were pretty comfortable there, making it easy to find a corner where I could grab a jacket from my suitcase, drape it over me and stretch myself out. It looked normal at first, since most people in the airport were carrying suitcases, too. I could just be a traveler waiting for a delayed flight for all anyone knew.

The security guards usually didn't buy it, though. As soon as I'd get comfortable, the hard wood of a nightstick would bang against the bench and a stern, cold voice would tell me to buy something or leave. After getting booted out of several spots, the officers would lose their patience and make me exit the premises while standing at the door to make sure I didn't come back in again.

Then, I'd use my shuttle pass to make my way over to the Amtrak station downtown. I liked it better there, anyway. It had much more traffic and I could watch people come in and out - especially all the pretty girls rushing back and forth.

Fortunately for me, it was Christmastime, the "feel-good" holiday season. This was the time of year where people were more generous to peddlers and solicitors. I would walk the streets asking strangers for money, getting dollars here and there - just enough to squeeze by. One time, a woman reached into her purse, pulled out a ten-dollar bill and handed it to me. Shocked, but grateful, I made plans to once again visit my new hangout - the Amtrak station.

The Philadelphia train station was a magnificent piece of architectural design. I would sit for hours admiring the high ceilings and detailed awnings. It was a huge place that had all kinds of stores, from bookstores to candy shops. I loved to hang around the candy shops. There was one that made fresh fudge. The smell of chocolate intoxicated me and I couldn't resist spending most of my pocket change there.

Meanwhile, *The Microchip* was telling me to sit and watch.

I did what it told me to, grabbing a spot on a bench. I'd scan the faces of passers-by as they rushed to and fro to catch their train or a cab to go home. I'd spot an old, white guy with a bald head and white beard bustle by and smile at me.

The chip said: *You're winning.*

Next, a middle-aged, black woman with dreadlocks would streak by with her elegant sweater-wrap coat flowing behind her. Her facial expression would be serious looking. She didn't even notice me.

The chip said: *Wait. You're losing.*

"Losing what?" I wanted to know. "What are we talking about here?"

The case, stupid. It fired back. *The lawsuit. They all know. Look for the clues. Agents are anybody and everybody.*

So I sat on a bench stuffing fudge chunks into my mouth, watching people for clues. I needed them to tell me whether I was making progress in my class-action suit or not. With each person that passed by, the answers kept changing: *yes, no, good job, terrible, win, lose* ... and around and around I went on the mental merry-go-round.

The pressure kept building up inside until the only way to release it was to face an agent head-on. I spotted an older man in business attire making his way across the floor when *The Microchip* told me that he was *the one*. It became necessary for me to take this undercover agent to task.

"YOU!" I pushed through the crowd and pointed at him. "LET ME GO, LET ME GO! TELL YOUR PEOPLE TO LET ME GO!!!" After all, I was the one who was there to save his people. *I* was the one who was sacrificing *MY* life for the cause, with these damn agents and lawyers following my every move...

He froze in his tracks and gave me a look that said, "O-o-okay lunatic," and kept going.

I sat down again, relieved that I had obeyed my orders. The pressure building up inside my head was less intense afterward.

I was homeless, but far from alone. In fact, I had stumbled onto a whole world of people ignored by everyone in plain sight. The streets had its own culture - very competitive and even dangerous because it was all about survival of the fittest. The good news: the other homeless guys were my allies in disguise, also fighting against the establishment. Lucky for me, I made friends with the right people - people who safeguarded me from getting raped or beat up. I did get robbed though. I lost my suitcase - I had it at the airport one day and the next, I didn't.

While "kickin' it" on the benches with my new street friends, I would get the scoop on survival. They'd give me their five-star ratings on the best shelters to get food and a hot shower. Usually, their recommendations were spot-on and hands-down the best grub you could ever get at a place like that. But sometimes the suggestions would be way off and the food unfit for dogs. Or the place would be overcrowded or just really gross. Other times they would point me in the direction and I would get lost on my way there, wandering around until I ran into some random shelter.

I'm not sure how I ended up at the local mall on this particular day, but I decided to call my cousin, Nanu – the same cousin that came down to see me at the hotel. He was the son of my father's other brother. I waited for him at the main entrance and hobbled over to the car when he pulled up. I got in and we were off.

"So do you want to go to your house or mine?" he asked.

I wasn't sure. I was too busy trying to size him up. He very well could be working for the legal firm or the FBI. I also thought about my mom's delicious food and how I missed it … then again, the agents were probably still there. Who knew what they and my parents had been planning for me while I was gone? Didn't they know I was on a mission here? The world needed my help...

"So?" Nanu took his eyes off the road to look at me. "What do you want to do?"

I felt my emotions rise up within me as I realized he was being sympathetic to my dilemma. He was acknowledging what *The Man* had put me through and was offering me a way out by staying with him. Maybe he was an ally after all...

I'd been on the streets for about a month and a half. It was time to go where my mom's cooking was.

It was a relief to have a hot shower and a warm bed to sleep in again. The smell of mom's food was like heaven to my nostrils and I scarfed it down like there wasn't any more coming down the pike. Being on the streets will do that to you. You never knew where your next hot meal, hot shower or warm sleeping place would come from.

Of course, it wasn't long before *The Man* started in on me again. He showed me the bill that came to him and how I had maxed out the card. Then he wanted to know about a rental car and some other significant purchases, being that he was the one held responsible. He also seemed to think I had fallen in with the wrong crowd and was using drugs. Not only that, but his displeasure was compounded by the fact that I was right back where I started. I was the same after I returned as before I left and *The Man* was frustrated. Mom was worried. Sleeping in one day was fine. But two, three, five, ten days in a row of doing nothing became a concern.

9

Raging Against the Machine

After my homeless days were over, life became a blur. I found myself constantly in and out of the hospital's mental ward. With each visit I'd lose more and more of my grip on reality.

It was a vicious cycle: I'd be a couch potato for a while, then *The Microchip* would kick in and I would find myself under restraints in the emergency room. They would pump me full of drugs. A few days would pass and I'd get heavily sedated and be under control. Then they would send me home to follow up with the outpatient clinic, which I never did. I was certain they were part of the conspiracy and were trying to poison me. Just like the hospital stays earlier, it just went around and around like this.

I'd been diagnosed with paranoid schizophrenia, but no one in my family understood what that was. I didn't accept that there was anything wrong with me and Mom and Dad couldn't monitor me and make me stick to the regimen because they were in denial themselves. When my behavior would get extreme, they'd do the necessary damage control and pick up the pieces. It was all they really could do. I believe they felt really helpless and afraid to talk about it for fear of not having an answer to make things better. Once the nightmare of my hospital stay would end, so would the discussion. For the first few days they'd make me take my meds, but after a few weeks things would always fade back into the old family routine. *The Man* would forget about seeing me delusional and would start yelling at me again.

The medications were a huge issue of contention between us. He would see my pill bottle on the counter, still half-full after two months and would yell at me to take them. But *The Genetic Microchip* was shooting sparks everywhere. No thought of mine was safe, not even from him. *The Genetic Microchip* said the meds were just another way that the powers that be were trying to kill me. And I wasn't about to give them that opportunity. There was too much at stake. The world needed me to stand up for them in court.

The Man was frustrated, but *The Undercover Sialkot Indian Artist* saw I was hurting. He brought me a very special gift while I was away at one of my hospital stays. Depressed and glued to the couch, I was flipping channels with the remote when *Dad* came in holding the most beautiful puppy I had ever seen. She was soft and furry with shiny, golden hair. Our old dog had died years before and we never got another one. Now there was a new puppy to love. I named her Sasha.

My life shifted meaning at that very moment - the same way *Dad's* did that morning at the well after his mother had passed. I feel as if I could write a whole book on Sasha alone. At my darkest hour, that little puppy lit up my world. There were - and are - no words to describe the impact she has had on my life and what motivation she gave me to push on. Now there was someone who needed me, a reason for me to get up in the morning.

One night, sitting on the couch with Sasha, *The Microchip* had an idea. I was in a real funk that night. Sasha had been biting on my feet and it hurt, but the pain was the only thing that reminded me I was still alive. Then suddenly it hit me: *The Genetic Microchip* had the answer of how I was going to win my law suit.

I grabbed the nearest set of keys, took one of my parent's cars and headed downtown to the local hospital. If I wanted to win my lawsuit I was going to have to take drastic action. I parked the car and walked to the front desk of the emergency room with a new declaration:

"I'm going to kill myself!"

I thought if it was documented that I tried to commit suicide then it would incur damages and win me the lawsuit. Then the lawyers would know they pushed me over the edge and the world would see their corrupt ways. In my mind, I wasn't actually going to outright kill myself, but somebody had to make some kind of sacrifice on behalf of the oppressed masses.

The girl behind the desk freaked out and immediately called for help. It wasn't long before I was strapped down and being ushered into the back of an ambulance. We were on our way to the mental clinic. As I laid there on the gurney staring at the ceiling there was only one thing on my mind:

Warren Buffett.

While on the ride in the ambulance, *The Microchip* picked up the signals from the conference. I was the topic of discussion. Seated among the roundtables were Warren, "Harry" (my old boss from Park Avenue), Johnny Cochran, Donald Trump, a long list of CEOs, Supreme Court judges, politicians and celebrity figures - all discussing the lawsuit and what to do about me. I began to panic.

"GOD! HELP ME GAH-AHAUD!!!" I screamed in agony, arching my body against the harnesses in a mix of defiance and desperation. The EMT worker tried to calm me down, but to no avail. He rushed over and used his body weight to pin my right side down. Suddenly I felt pressure on the inside of my elbow followed by a sharp burst of pain as he plunged a long needle full of liquid into my arm. I cried out for him to

Murder and Misunderstanding

stop, but after a few seconds the sharp sensation dwindled down to a warm tingle that spread slowly throughout my body.

By the time we pulled up to the clinic I was sweating and panicky, but the drugs had diffused into my brain, causing my heart to beat slower. I became calmer. Now I was in a weird state of awareness. I was wide awake and comatose at the same time, trapped inside a drooping, numb body - only able to observe the outside world as an innocent bystander.

They rolled me out of the ambulance and into the sliding glass doors of the emergency room for the intake process. It was a huge building, one of the well-known mental health clinics in the area. As the gurney glided through the halls, I watched white ceiling tiles whisk by through drooping eyelids. The rolling movement was soothing to me and I just laid there quiet.

Finally we stopped and I found myself in what looked like a temporary room with a curtain. The EMTs unstrapped my wrists and ankles, moved me onto the hospital bed and strapped my hands and feet again. I didn't resist. I stared into the bright fluorescent lights, which seemed like white beams from heaven enveloping me. Maybe I was crossing over. Maybe God had answered me in the ambulance...

"Hello? Can you hear me?" A beautiful angel with a red halo appeared and was standing over me. I noticed the angel had a pen and clipboard. Trying to make sure I was seeing correctly, I blinked hard to clear my head and opened my eyes again. There stood a hot, redhead girl asking me questions about insurance.

I don't know what I said or did, but, as if in a dream, the scene changed and I was sitting in the same room with an older woman doctor. As she was speaking, I tried to make sense of who she might be. At first, I thought she was Muslim, but slowly I began to recognize her accent as

Russian. She was asking me questions and I was answering them. I couldn't believe how well she could read my thoughts. Maybe it was the stuff the medic gave me, like some kind of truth serum. Everything felt surreal. The room was like a mirage, pulsating back and forth in waves.

Once I was checked in, they placed me in a room upstairs by myself. The doctor ordered that I be put on serious meds. The place didn't have bars on the windows or padded walls. It was just a clinic, leaving me free to do whatever I wanted once the nurse left the room. I'd pretend to swallow my pills while she was there then spit them down the toilet once she was gone. After maybe a week or two of this routine, while the toilet was flushing this particular day, I stopped to look at myself in the bathroom mirror.

You're being reborn, The Pope said.

The Pope was sending signals through the satellites and they were bouncing his ideas down to me right there in the bathroom. I locked the door and began filling the bathtub with warm water. It was time to be baptized and born again.

After peeling my clothes off, I slowly eased myself into the tub. I sucked in the biggest breath I could manage and completely immersed myself underwater. The "glub" sound of the water swallowing my head cut off my hearing as I sank to the bottom.

The Pope sent me a second message, telling me to stay underwater until I died and was resurrected. At that moment, being reborn meant I had to die and be raised from the dead. But I couldn't let go. My head rested on the bottom of the tub with the drain hole against the base of my skull. My eyes forced themselves open and little bubbles escaped my pressed lips, floating to the surface of the water. The room waved back and forth as I looked up at the ceiling. I tried to die. I tried to inhale the water and let it fill my lungs. But my body was losing the battle and instincts and reflexes were winning. Gasping, I surged out of the water in a sitting position. I wiped the wet strands of hair from my eyes as I continued to gulp air into my lungs. I had failed my assignment.

Looking back, given my earlier statement that I was going to kill myself, I don't know why there weren't more precautions taken. Maybe they thought the medications were working, I don't know.

After the tub incident, I secretly decided that it wasn't my fault. Perhaps baptism wasn't the way to be reborn. Maybe it was something else I needed to do. Every day, when the nurse came in with the meds I took them or, more often than not, hid them under my tongue and spit them out when she was gone. I still didn't think there was anything wrong with me, so why should I take these medications?

This was supposed to be my last time in a place like this. Dad told me on one of his visits. I was sitting in the communal kitchen area when he arrived. A few days or weeks had passed since I was first admitted. In the mental clinic, one can never be sure of time. It had to have been a while because he came on his own carrying some home-cooked, Indian food my mother had made for me. Seeing how far out there I was, it must have broken his heart. He loved me, he just didn't know how to show it. Instead he kept repeating, "I promise it's your last time, I promise this is your last time..." I believe if love and desire alone could have made it true, it would have been my last time. What neither of us knew was that this wasn't the last time. It was only the beginning.

10

A New Beginning

After I no longer seemed to be suicidal, they sent me home on Clozaril, a drug originally introduced in the seventies, but not approved in the US until 1990 as an option for treatment-resistant forms of schizophrenia. I became a zombie. I drooled both when I was awake and after it made me pass out. When I came back to consciousness there would be slobber all over the pillow. It also eroded my white blood cell count, so I had to get blood work done once a week. They said that I would get used to it, but I didn't. The hell in between was too much.

Unlike the other times I had been sent home from the hospital, instead of just vegging out on the sofa, I found myself becoming increasingly interested in alternative healing. Clozaril was a nightmare and I kept thinking there had to be a better way to live. The paranoia and delusions seemed to be under control, but I was so sedated that everyday activities were becoming miracles to accomplish. I slept most of the time. All I did was sleep and eat, which began to take its toll on my body. The pounds crept on daily, it seemed. Before I knew it, my once lean and muscular physique was now that of a puffy brown marshmallow.

I, again, started hiding the pills Mom brought for me. When *The Man* asked if I took my medicine I said yes, just to get him off my case. With each refusal, I began to gain some semblance of coherent thought again -

enough to begin researching alternative therapies on the internet. Initially, my intent was to find alternatives to pharmaceutical drugs. Anything had to be better than Clozaril.

Surfing the net brought my attention to a whole bunch of topics. A lot of the information I found just described the symptoms of schizophrenia. But there was other information that talked about "complementary therapies" such as eliminating certain things from the diet, herbal supplements, and vitamin therapy. These posed problems, though. Mom wasn't going to change her menu after all of these years and I wasn't sure I even wanted her to. Plus, I was broke and I knew *The Man* wasn't interested in giving me money to buy a supply of very expensive supplements every month. It was new territory and I couldn't even be sure they would work anyway. Meanwhile, my dream team, who consisted of my doctor and my therapist, were split down the middle. "Doc" insisted on me taking the drugs and my therapist agreed with my decision to seek out other avenues of recovery. My therapist's opinion was, at least, a relief, because, as a guy in his early 20s, I couldn't imagine being a drooling marshmallow with my whole life ahead of me.

I became intrigued with the idea of taking control of my life again. I don't know that I ever had control of it in the first place, but now was the time I could make my own decisions. My quest led me to a website talking about the healing benefits of meditation. It even mentioned being able to heal the mind - and my brain definitely needed healing. The website had a toll-free number to get more information. I called it with eager anticipation. The person who answered the phone was perky and upbeat. I don't remember the conversation, except that he referred me to a website for a meditation school - what I'll call "The University".

"The University" website was a colorful virtual brochure lined with airbrushed photos of smiling faces under a banner that read, "A consciousness-based education". Underneath was an offer for a free orientation weekend for prospective students. I called the 800 number.

The person on the phone promised me a travel voucher for a three-day weekend visit. It was a win-win situation. Excited, I ran the idea by my therapist during one of our buffet sessions. He thought it was a great idea. I could use a break from the madness, he said. Not only that, it was a free vacation as far as I was concerned.

I told my parents about the school and the free weekend orientation. The travel voucher they promised was more like a reimbursement thing it seemed, so I asked *The Man* for the plane ticket money. He gave it to me. I think he and Mom were just glad to see some life within their son again. I don't think they completely understood, but at least I was trying to go back to school. I made arrangements for a flight, filled out the school registration forms and I was on my way.

When I exited the small airport, a thirty-something year old, white guy was leaning against the hood of a used Subaru Outback waiting for me. I think he worked for the school. He recognized me as his pick-up, so we jumped in the car and were off to my latest getaway.

The ride was filled with casual, upbeat conversation. As the cornfields and open grassland rolled by my window, I relaxed and inhaled deeply. Despite the hint of manure in the air, it was great to be away. Maybe I could start over. Maybe I could walk away from my mission to save mankind and de-activate *The Genetic Microchip* once and for all.

After about 30 minutes, we arrived at the campus, a city unto itself. It was rural and the buildings were spaced out between long stretches of finely manicured lawns. I was impressed with the vedic architecture everywhere. In Hindu culture, "vedic architecture" means the buildings are designed in a way to harmonize universal principles with natural law. For instance, at "The University," the buildings were built facing east in order to maximize the energy and beauty of the rising sun. It really appealed to me. The guy pulled up to the administration building and dropped me off.

Murder and Misunderstanding

The admissions office was in plain sight and easy to find. From the minute I walked in, the staff members were all very friendly. Everyone seemed happy to see me. I took a seat with one of the counselors. It was a small office full of the comforting amenities of home. There was a real family-vibe in the air. Looking around, I noticed there were people of different ages and ethnicities. A twenty-something, Indian girl whisked by, shooting a smile at me and the counselor, who was doing my paperwork. Voices of what sounded like an older, white male and female buzzed in the back office. A black man gave an Asian co-worker a file by the water cooler as they discussed the contents inside. The others were all smiling and also very friendly.

A few minutes later, the man whose voice I had heard in the back entered the area where I was sitting and filling out forms for my voucher. He was Caucasian, a broad shouldered man with graying hair and a wide smile. He said hello and we struck up a conversation. I discovered he was formerly in the Air Force and now he and his wife were in the higher education business together.

After I got my dorm room key, I was introduced to my tour guide. He was another thirty-something-year-old, white guy who was very cheerful and happy to see me. He also seemed to know the campus like the back of his hand. Our first stop was my dorm room. My heart sank when he pointed out where I would be staying. It was an old building under construction. I went upstairs and unloaded my luggage while the tour guide waited downstairs.

Next were the classroom halls. The red brick and mortar buildings were reminiscent of my days at Pace. The guide led me into a classroom that looked like a science lab. The professor was smiling and friendly and was more than happy to show me one of the devices he was using. It looked like a yarmulke with lots of wires coming out of it. He said that he used this hat to measure the brain wave activity of students while they were meditating. According to him, the cap provided scientific proof that meditation and its effects were real. Apparently the subjects who were meditating had brain waves that slowed dramatically compared to beforehand. The professor spent the next few minutes showing me images of brain scans to give me a visual of what he was describing.

We proceeded to make our way across the well-manicured landscape until we reached a round building known as "The Dome". It loomed majestically over us, reminding me of a giant Faberge egg.

When we went inside, there were a bunch of chairs and musical recorders lying beside each seat. My guide explained that it was summer break, which was why there were no students inside. He went on to say that "The Dome" was where the most advanced spiritual meditation achievers practiced their levitation techniques.

Next he showed me the organic kitchen in the cafeteria. Then we visited "The University's" school of medicine. Once inside, I was introduced to an Indian medical professor who was in one of the labs. He was really nice as well. The doctor's assistant was there, too - another girl that I connected with personality-wise (unfortunately, she was engaged to some guy). She began explaining something called "pulse-diagnosis." This was supposedly a technique used to diagnose diseases and conditions by measuring someone's pulse. She used an example of a woman who came to her not feeling well and how she was able to diagnose her pregnancy just by reading her pulse.

That night I had a hard time falling asleep in the old-looking dorm. To me it was a new place with new sounds and new smells. The furniture was shabby and my bed was uncomfortable, but I lay there, staring at the ceiling, my mind racing at full speed. Unsure of what to make of all the new things I'd seen that day, I decided to get some sleep. The next day was a new day and I had to be up early to continue the weekend itinerary.

Murder and Misunderstanding

On Saturday, I met some of the students at the school. One was a nerdy black guy named "Steve" who invited me to a party off campus. I didn't have a car, so "Steve" offered me a ride. Thinking back to my partying days at Pace, I was mentally prepping my mind for a rockin' good time.

What I walked into was the strangest Saturday night party I had ever attended. It was at a small, one-bedroom apartment several miles away from campus. A few guests were already there when we arrived. They were super-friendly and glad to see us. But instead of a beer keg in the corner, there was a raw veggie platter. Girls going wild were replaced with people sipping on tea and standing around talking. There was no weed smoke in the air, only the soft hum of hippie tunes on the CD player. It looked weird to me at first, but since I was a people person, it was easy to make the social adjustment. Actually, this appealed to me even more because these people were "walking the walk" with this conscious living thing. I could tell by the way the guys joked around with each other that it was a close-knit group. They were older - maybe in their late twenties to mid-thirties, and seemed more mature than I was at the time. Overall it was a pleasant experience with pleasant people. Later that night, one of the guys dropped me off at my dorm and I headed up to bed.

The last night of the weekend rolled around and the prospective students were invited to a "meet-n-greet" banquet. The school seemed to pull out all the stops for us, with the tables decorated with candles, the best china and maroon tablecloths. The event was held in one of the dining halls on campus. I took my place at the head table with the other orientation students and tucked in my napkin. The organic food being served looked fresh and healthy. Once again, I looked around the room at the sea of smiling faces wearing nametags. The ex-Air Force pilot and his wife were at my table dressed like they were going out to a nice restaurant. It seemed as if they were trying to make me feel comfortable.

Shubi S.

The pilot was in an even more jovial mood than when we had met at the admissions office.

"I'm not one to tell people what to do, but you should really come here," he said, crunching raw vegetables between his large white teeth. Then his wife jumped in. "It's the best four years you'll ever spend. Here there is so much more than a regular education - true education is about consciousness."

Another professor stopped by the table, patted my shoulder and shook my hand. After he left, the wife continued. "There's no better place for you to be right now, Shubi. Here you will learn meditation, how to live a healthy lifestyle - all while taking a marketable major."

"That sounds cool," I said, taking another bite out of the raw green salad on my plate, thinking about the hot Indian meal my mother was probably making back home. I hadn't come to any definite conclusions just yet, but subconsciously I already knew that I had made up my mind that they were right.

11

The University

"The University" visit had been a positive experience. It'd made me feel good. They'd given me a purpose to exist. That weekend, I had discovered the possibility of things like transcendental meditation. Now I could exist beyond my current reality. I was Hindu, so meditation was normal in my family. But I was also American - and such things were watered down by my immersion in western culture. Tapping into my sub-consciousness and being one with the world ... it was cool for me. They'd made me feel special, like I would be enlightened. All this resonated with *The Genetic Microchip*. I was a superhero meant to save mankind and "The University" was the perfect training ground for me to do it.

When *The Man* picked me up at the airport, I was excited. As usual, he just shook his head and laughed mockingly at my enthusiasm. On the ride home he insisted that I review the situation with my therapist - the old, partially blind hippie psychotherapist.

I was confident that I wanted to go to "The University", but I needed this guy to sign off on it and convince my parents. They would have to let me go if a mental health professional gave me the green light. And that was exactly what they did. In fact, "Doc" said it would be good for me, since I would be in a new place. A change of scene and a fresh start was just what I needed. Ever since the clinic, I had been on autopilot. I had slipped back into a very mild remission, but my half-blind therapist was oblivious to it. There was no other viable option at the time. I was unproductive, sitting around the house all day, so anything was worth a shot. My folks couldn't argue with his prognosis, so when September rolled around I was packed and off to the Midwest to begin my new path.

~

When I exited the airport this time, like when I had gone for the orientation, there stood the same thirty-something-year-old, white guy leaning against the same used Subaru Hatchback. But this time he wasn't so friendly. On the way to campus, he informed me of the 40 dollar car fare. "Car fare?" I said in disbelief. He didn't ask for car fare last time. Now he had his hand out as if this was the way it was all along.

He dropped me off at the administration building (after we stopped at an ATM so I could pay him), so I could settle my financial aid and get my room key. Back home, I had tried to get everything lined up in advance, but the counselor told me not to worry. He said I could do it when I arrived in September and that they would take good care of me.

In the admissions office, it was less family-like and more about business. The small space which once felt homey and personal was now a hustling-bustling atmosphere. It was also time for bad news. The financial aid didn't cover everything, so I had to fill out the paperwork for a student loan. I didn't understand the whole procedure. All I knew was that the lady handed me a bunch of long forms. I filled them out, signed my name on the dotted line and the next thing I knew, I was in school.

I was told by the former Air Force pilot-turned-admissions director that he was going to be my Transcendental Meditation (TM) instructor. I also found out that taking TM wasn't optional - according to the counselor it was mandatory in order to be enrolled. I didn't understand why, since business was my major. On top of this, because my loans hadn't been processed yet, I had to cough up 1000 dollars up-front as a deposit. Once again, I was in a jam; and once again, only one person could save me. I called home to get the money. *The Man* was irritated, but he settled the fee anyway. He mailed them a check, so I would be clear in 5-7 business days. This would mean I would miss the first day of classes.

As I walked to my dorm, I was sad to see that it was still under construction - a stark contrast to the girl's dorm next door, which was much nicer and more modern with state-of-the art amenities. Pulling my suitcases up the stairs, I opened the door to a single occupancy room. I dropped my stuff and took a quick look around. The room was small with one little window, a cast-iron steam radiator under it, a twin bed on one wall and a small desk attached to the opposite wall. Not the typical Pace dorm room, even with the small, sub-par settings of New York living space. It was okay, I told myself. At least I was free of *The Man* and was starting my new path.

Meanwhile, I discovered more bad news. Apparently, I had to take a semester of foundational courses before I could begin the business curriculum. Those courses included "Creative Science of Intelligence" (commonly referred to as CSI), "Teaching for Enlightenment" and another class on the basic principles of meditation.

By the time *The Man's* check arrived, classes had already started and I had to be brought up to speed on what I missed. I met with the ex-Air Force pilot during his office hours. He welcomed me into his lavish, corner office right before class and gently closed the door behind him.

His space had that "zen" feeling to it. There was a huge oak desk, a panoramic view of the campus and a lot of New Age pictures on the wall. The largest picture was of the founder of "The University"- the yogi

Shubi S.

master - an older Indian guy sitting cross-legged in a yoga posture. There were chimes on his desk and a small tabletop rock fountain which softly trickled water down its smooth edges over and over again. He explained that we would be going to another spot in the building to perform meditation since I missed the first session.

I followed him to a tiny room where it was quiet and the air was thick with incense. The walls were decorated with symbols and figurines of Indian culture. We got down on the floor, facing each other and crossed our legs. He told me we were doing *Puja*, which was cool because I was already familiar with it. *Puja* was a meditation practice my family had done when I was growing up. My mom was the most consistent, kneeling before the god and goddess statues and singing songs. With *Puja,* people had different ways of honoring the gods - my mom sang songs, others placed food before the statues along with other things in the spirit of honor and sacrifice. The ex-pilot pulled out one of the many candles lined up against the wall and sat it in between us. He lit it. Then he started chanting and speaking words in *Sanskrit.* (Sanskrit is a pseudo-ancient language that Indian people respect, while also recognizing its origins come from Great Britain invading Indian territory centuries ago).

I liked the ex-pilot. He seemed like a really nice guy who meant well, but his chanting sounded fake to me. It was obvious that this wasn't his native culture and his words sounded far from authentic. My family's language is based in Hindi, so I wasn't able to understand what he was saying, except for a few Hindu words. With the monotone vibration of his voice and the hypnotic energy inside the four walls, I could feel myself slowly slipping. I kept opening my eyes to feel stable again. Each time I did, I noticed that the candle light was flickering nonstop, even though there were no open windows and we were sitting perfectly still. Sitting cross-legged with both wrists resting against his two knees, the ex-pilot's eyes remained closed the entire time while his thin lips were rapidly moving in line with the non-stop stream of enunciated sounds escaping them. A few minutes of chanting passed and I felt my mind lock into a state of confusion. It felt like there was a muscle cramp in my brain. What was happening…?

"Shubi."

I opened my eyes again.

"I want you to remember this word: Icine".

There we were, sitting on the floor like two little boys sharing secrets in summer camp. His "zen-ness" suddenly morphed into a face only his military subordinates could love. He'd already given the other kids in my class the word. He told me that "Icine" was strictly patented by law and warned me about using the word outside of "The University". "Icine" was NEVER to be disclosed to outsiders, EVER.

I wasn't exactly sure how you could own a word, but, seeing his intensity, I nodded my head in agreement and said that I understood. He blew the candle out; we stood up and went back to his office. It was almost time for class, so we walked over to "The Dome" together.

The classroom had some serious ambiance - way nicer than my sub-par dorm room. It was state-of-the-art vedic with comfortable chairs, lush green plants and golden rays of sunshine streaming in from the angled glass ceiling panels. The floor was carpeted and the comfy chairs were everywhere. Since it was a meditation class, we could sleep on the chairs, the floor, or wherever we wanted during these spiritual "naptimes".

The professor believed in the power of numbers. So if two people were meditating at the same time, then the brainwaves were combined, amplifying each other. And with a classroom of 20 or more, the power was exponential. These were people who believed that a bunch of students and faculty chaperones could go to Wall Street and change the stock prices just by group meditation alone. In fact, they made the newspaper headlines once or twice with their radical Wall Street demonstrations. I learned fast that these courses were more theoretical and abstract than what I was used to. There were no textbooks or exams - just class participation, papers and attendance.

For the first month, everything felt normal. I was in school again and on my own away from home - but this time around I wasn't binging on alcohol and getting my girlfriend pregnant. Now, I was being enlightened. There was something about this "higher learning" that was magical. Levitation, meditation, higher sciences, special foods ... it felt as if I was part of an elite experience. It felt as if I *was* elite - a real superhero, confirming my past suspicions that I was out to save the world. And with all the meditation techniques I was learning, I would be able to cancel out the sparks of *The Microchip* once and for all. And for a while, I managed to keep the sparks under wraps. I would see and hear things that made me trippy, but was able to manage it enough to get by. But that could only last for so long.

Thoughts of the conspiracy started creeping back into my head. I had completely stopped taking the Clozaril and soon I was secretly waiting to see what was going to happen in my life. No one knew I was again holding on for this big event to take place. I knew something cataclysmic always had to happen before the superhero could go into action. So, I was on guard every day, waiting for the big event to show up and reveal itself. Everywhere I went, there were ideas and subliminal references being thrown at me once more.

A guy would pass me by in the hallway and say, "Hey buddy, how's it goin' today?"

I'd hear, "Go here and do that."

The cafeteria lady would smile at me while serving me food at the dining hall counter.

I saw her signaling me to keep my eyes open and watch out for clues.

Every day became about looking for clues telling me what to do next. A lot of these clues were in class. Then, one day, *The Genetic Microchip* started going haywire during Transcendental Meditation. The ex-Air Force pilot was in the middle of his lecture when I raised my hand to tell him that I needed to go to the medical office right away. "Right now?" he responded in disbelief, as my classmates turned in unison to look at me. "Can't you wait until class is over?"

"Uh - no." I barely got the words out. He didn't have a clue about what he was asking me to do. It wasn't even an option to wait with *The Microchip* shooting sparks everywhere. I had been in this situation before and it wasn't good. Before he could respond, I grabbed my backpack and left. My next stop was the vedic-style hospital on campus. Soon, I was inside the doctor's office, anxious and unsure of what was going to happen in this new unfamiliar place. Back home, the routine had become simple: lose control, go to the hospital. Here, it was just me and the girl at the front desk. *The Man* wasn't around to swoop in and pull me back from the edge.

The receptionist handed me some medical forms and told me to have a seat while I was waiting to be seen. I tried hard to focus my attention on answering the questions, but the form was too long and the letters seemed too small.

My hand was trembling as I printed my name and other basic information. I flipped the sheet over only to see an endless list of things to be checked off: what diseases I had and what diseases I used to have. It then asked me to describe what symptoms I was experiencing. I checked the boxes that read "out of focus" and "delusions" - along with a host of other classic schizophrenic symptoms.

"The doctor is ready to see you now," the girl said.

"Dr. Smith" was an older, white man in his fifties or sixties. His office looked like any other doctor's office, but this time I didn't have to take off my clothes and put on some flimsy gown. He asked me to have a seat and placed two fingers on my wrist to take my pulse. I remembered the pulse diagnosis conversation with one of the campus doctors back during my orientation tour. My heart felt as if it was beating too fast while I tried to explain to him what I was feeling.

"Dr. Smith" let go of my wrist and listened intently for several minutes. Then he said:

"I want you to hum ... like a bee."

I looked at him to see if he was serious. He maintained a straight face. "Hum like a bee?" I said, frowning at him in pain. How ridiculous. But *The Genetic Microchip* was buzzing inside my head and I was panicky. The sounds were too loud for critical thinking. Okay, I decided. I'll hum ... anything to make the buzzing of *The Microchip* go away. So I pursed my lips together and forced the humming sound out of my throat, trying to sound like a bee. After a few repetitions, he seemed satisfied. He began telling me his thoughts.

As he was talking, the voices inside my head were so loud that I couldn't make out what he was saying. All the while, I kept grabbing my head. A piercing, deep pain seized my brain and I felt as if my head was going to explode. Unlike *The Man*, who didn't let the voices keep him from my brain's VIP space, "Doc" was fading away to a *wah-wah-wah* in the background.

Murder and Misunderstanding

I picked the conversation back up a few minutes later ... he was saying something about body types and how I was something called *vata* and *pitta*. He went to his desk and pulled out a sheet of paper which was a diet plan for my body type. My body was out of balance, so he told me to make sure I went to sleep before nine o'clock every night. He also prescribed me two oils and told me where to buy them - one to drop inside my nose and the other to rub on my back. This was what he called *Ayurvedic* treatment. As a Hindu, I was already familiar with it, but I never considered it could help me with *The Microchip*. He went into a whole speech about *doshas* - three substances called *vata, pitta* and *kapha*. According to him, the symptoms were the manifested stress of my mind and body and I needed to calm myself down.

"There are certain foods you must refrain from," he continued on matter-of-factly, ignoring the sight of me sitting there clutching my head. "Take the oils, apply them, and follow the regimen for the next few days. If that doesn't work, then we will use western medicine." I tried to focus again, watching him shuffle around the room preparing my file to hand to the nurse. It seemed this guy had everything down pat. I figured he must really know what he was doing.

An Indian girl who worked at the clinic offered to give me a ride to the health store since she had a car and was going there anyway. I took her up on her offer, bought the oils the doctor prescribed (which turned out to be pretty pricey) and she brought me back to my dorm, leaving me alone in my room with *The Microchip* once again. I dropped one of the medicines in my nose and as "Dr. Smith" had told me to do, I began humming like a bee. The humming aggravated *The Microchip* and it made the voices more pronounced, as if it were opening a channel for more voices to come in. I took my shirt off, rubbed the other oil on my back and, exhausted from the day's events, fell fast asleep.

Over the next few weeks I became more erratic. This time was different than the others, though. This time, I was falling off the cliff with no one to catch me and only some oils and a humming technique as treatment.

Every person I encountered was a potential enemy - someone who was secretly plotting behind my back. I became very snappy and was biting people's heads off. No one noticed, except to say things like, "Hey man, what the hell is your problem?" They must have thought I was just in a bad mood. But I wasn't. What I happened to be was someone losing touch with reality.

"Steve" - the nerdy, black guy who had taken me to my first party off campus - was my first victim. I threatened to slam his head against the sink. We were in the bathroom, which was a communal restroom shared by the whole floor. I was going in to take a shower while he was on his way out. He didn't miss a beat. He sent some slick comments my way. Because of my easy-going temperament, he was always making fun of me, calling me soft - among other things. At times, he could be really mean and that morning I had had more than enough of his bullshit. He didn't take being threatened too lightly, backing out of the room visibly shaken up. I thought he was going to tell the residential assistant in our dorm, but I never heard anything more from him after that.

The group of guys I tended to hang around with: "Mark", "Dennis", "Akbar", "Aaron" and "Martin" were becoming suspects.

First I accused "Dennis" of being a spy.

Then "Aaron" and I got into it in the parking lot.

"Martin" and I argued and I stopped speaking to him.

One by one, I alienated myself from my friends. Except for "Mark". He had a car and I didn't, so I rode shotgun with him a lot. "Mark" was the new "Noland" in my life. Our car rides always included conversations about real estate. He wanted to do the real estate thing.

Since my father had owned rental properties over the years, I would tell him what a hassle it was trying to get tenants to pay their rent and not tear the property apart.

One particular low point came when I was running around the student parking lot in circles. A cat was chasing me.

"There's no cat there, man," "Mark" kept saying.

I couldn't understand what he was talking about, the cat was right there in plain sight. All I could do was scream in terror as the black furry creature was trying to attack me. It had been following me all over campus. The lawyers were trying to win the case by planting this cat in the college parking lot to take me out.

Weeks had gone by (I think) and I hadn't returned to "Dr. Smith's" office. If humming and oils was all he had to offer, then, in my mind, I felt I was better on my own. Following his directions had really just exacerbated *The Microchip* and now it was on a rampage. Life became one, long, continuous loop - like a comic strip switching frames. I knew where I was at, yet I didn't. One minute I was running frantically away from a cat and the next I was sitting in class. Just like when a comic strip changes scenes, I was sliding from one scenario to the next not really aware of how I even got there.

The next place I found myself was my Transcendental Meditation class. This day, we were going to practice meditating in a dream state. Everyone settled into a chair or a spot on the floor to begin meditating. As people around me were drifting off to sleep, my eyes were wide open. I had to keep one eye open at all times. Someone was out to get me. The people I was bringing the lawsuit against knew I was at "The University" and they had to pull every trick in the book to bring me down. The old pilot kept repeating the secret word over and over, locking everyone into a meditative trance.

Shubi S.

"Icine"

I thought the worst was over after "Dr. Smith" and his odd suggestions. But now the piercing pain was in my head again.

The next class, the pilot had a video featuring "The Master" - the same Indian guy who was hanging up on the wall of his office. This man was some kind of spiritual guru who founded "The University" which also bore his name. As the camera zoomed in on his wrinkled brown face, I noticed something.

He winked. Yes, he was winking at me!

My head was pounding.

He kept acting jovial - smiling, nodding his head. And then he winked at me again.

"What does this mean?" I asked.

He's giving you the OK.

"Okay for what?"

For what?!? He's SAYING to do it.

I jumped out of my chair, frantically running my fingers through my hair. All eyes were on me as I briskly exited the dark room with the movie still running.

The hallway was empty and I paced back and forth, sweating, trying to come to grips with the decision I had to make.

I had to save my people. I had to save all dark, indigenous people from the iron fist of the Germans ... no, Jews ... or was it the Germans? I couldn't get a clear signal.

Murder and Misunderstanding

I looked outside the window at the end of the hall, trying to find any clues as to what I should do next. There they were, just as I thought. The lawyers - sitting in that same parked car, waiting for me right there in front of the building...

My next move was to go to the bathroom to figure things out. *The Microchip* wasn't sending me any direct signals. It was a filter, taking my thoughts and connecting them to people like *The Radiologist*, the lawyers and the other outsiders. I paced back and forth in the empty bathroom.

I began thinking about the journal I'd been keeping since the beginning of the semester. When I became overwhelmed with T*he Microchip's* signals, I had made it a habit to grab one of my black and white notebooks and scribble my thoughts down. I was trying to make order out of mental chaos by connecting the dots. Some nights I almost broke my pen because I was scribbling so feverishly. Boy, I wished I had my notebook right there and then. It was my only outlet for the pressure building up inside my skull.

I took a seat on one of the toilets and held my throbbing head, staring at the tiles neatly designed on the floor. The image of that notebook flooded my mind, all the pages filled with chicken scratch - my writings about people I was bringing a lawsuit against which included psychiatrists and therapists, the CEOs of companies like Disney, the pharmaceutical companies, Redstone, Viacom, and a whole bunch of other powerful public figures. *The Chip* was making connections between them and what I was seeing around me. It was bouncing the images back to my brain from the satellites. There was definitely a conspiracy going on. This wasn't just about the lawsuit. This was about the conspiracy *behind* the lawsuit.

Something had to be done. I had to take immediate action. All of these people in this school were agents working for *The Oppressors*.

Shubi S.

There was just one problem: I wasn't an aggressive person. Or violent. In fact, I was a big teddy bear who got along with everyone. So I didn't know what to do, except *The Microchip* was shooting sparks everywhere and had already given me my orders. I just wasn't sure if it was the right or wrong thing to do. My previous attempts at dismantling the lawsuit had failed. Mental ward vacations, suicide attempts ... I had to do something else.

The more I thought about it, the more confused I got. It was such a moment of angst, the deepest of inner conflict.

When I finally went back inside, the lights were up and the tape had ended. Everyone was talking about what they thought of the presentation.

"Dave" was sitting in the chair behind mine. He was sharing his opinion with the rest of the class.

I knew at that moment what I had to do.

12

Son of a Bitch

"YOU SON OF A BITCH!!!!!!"

I did it. Grabbing "Dave's" head, I put him in a headlock, snatched the pen out of his hand and thrust it toward him. He put his other hand up and deflected the blow, causing me to puncture his cheek. People in the room were in shock. No one was more in shock than "Dave," who was on one knee holding his face. Somebody pulled me off of him and both of the teachers (the pilot had another woman assisting him with the class) rushed me outside. Someone hurried to "Dave's" side with something for his face as I was being pushed into another classroom across the hall.

While "Dave" was bleeding and exasperated, I was angry and my pulse was racing at top speed. I did it. And now these agents were trying to do damage control.

"*Why did you do that?!*" the old pilot demanded.

I was unresponsive. I didn't look directly at him. I knew it was best for me to keep my mouth shut with these agents trying to catch me in my own trap.

He left the room for what seemed like a really long time. I heard some frantic discussion from the hallway and he returned with "Dave", leading him by the shoulder to where I was seated.

"You need to apologize," the ex-pilot said.

As he was talking, I looked at his eyes trying to read his thoughts. All I could hear was the sound of *The Microchip*. I felt like I was underwater.

"So, are you going to apologize?" he reiterated, adjusting his eyeglasses.

I shrugged haphazardly. He was an agent, so I decided to just go along with it, to play the game. I looked at "Dave" who was standing there looking disgruntled. He was taking in deep heaving breaths, with the ex-pilot's long hand resting on his shoulder to keep him calm. Feeling all eyes bearing down on me in scrutiny, I stood up and did the deed.

Once the words "I'm sorry" escaped my lips, there was a collective sigh of relief that filled the room. I could tell they wanted the situation to be over with, whether or not I was being sincere. But I was sincere - sincerely convinced that they were all conspiring against me.

Everything seemed to go back to normal after that. In fact, it was well known that "The Dome" had a reputation for fights breaking out between students due to the high level of stress release during meditation sessions. So instead of sounding the alarm, the professors told everyone things were fine. Now, the other kids were talking and laughing again in the TM room. Things seemed calm again, but it was obvious that class was ending early that day.

I was picking up my backpack to leave when "Stan" tapped my shoulder. "Stan" was the school dean of men. I think the ex-Air Force pilot ran back to his office to call him while they made me wait in the other room. "Stan" was a tall, slender, soft-spoken German guy with an angled jawline and tousled brown hair. His brown eyes seemed very gentle and calm as he spoke and patted me on the shoulder. He was wearing a v-neck sweater over a button-up shirt with creased slacks.

Another agent, I decided, but I couldn't hide my vulnerabilities this time around. The sweat was drenching the hair on my forehead as my dilated pupils stared into his.

In a fatherly tone, "Stan" reassured me it had been a stressful day and that I needed to rest. He invited me to his place for a few hours to chill out and cool down. Looking back, I think it might have been more of a command than a suggestion, but I was pretty disoriented and paranoid and went along without any resistance.

His place was a small, one-bedroom apartment on the second or third floor. When he unlocked the door I walked into the living room, which was to the right-hand side. The wall to the left was a closet. We were standing inside a modestly-decorated living room which opened up to a tiny kitchen area.

"Stan" let me use his phone to call *The Man*. My father couldn't have been prepared to hear what I had to tell him. I may have been a huge disappointment, but I was the gentlest soul he'd ever known.

Mom picked up. She sounded happy to hear from me, but instantly knew something was wrong. While she was talking, I had a quick trip down memory lane. Ironically, I had played the role of peacemaker between two other guys about to get into a fight earlier that week. I came outside of the dorm just in time to see "Wesley"- a half-German, half-Indian kid - shoving around a little guy half his size.

"Hey chill, man," I told him. "You need to think this through - your ass is gonna get suspended."

"What's wrong?" Mom wanted to know. "What is it, Shubi?"

I avoided going into detail about why I was calling by saying I was in trouble and needed to talk to Dad right away. As her voice echoed through the house calling Dad's name, I wondered what in the hell I was going to say to him. How could I tell him the truth about me handling my business as a superhero? Or that I was protecting myself against the class-action lawsuit that had the lawyers watching my every move? How did I know he wasn't in on it, too?

Dad got on the line with that tone in his voice again - that one that sent chills up my spine. Shaking in my boots, I told him I had attacked someone. As he was freaking out on the other end of the phone, my mind was once again drifting down memory lane. That morning was when I should have known it was going to be a bad day. I got into a fight with "Aaron" in the parking lot.

"Fuck you, man!" he was fuming.

"Fuck you!" I fired back, not considering "Aaron's" huge frame. He kept talking about how he was a millionaire and I was tired of it. I was getting out of "Mark's" car to head for class when he pulled in to the parking space next to us. Unprovoked, I began firing cuss words at him before he even turned off the car engine. I was pissed, being that he - like the black cat – had been stalking me around campus on behalf of the lawyers.

I didn't like him because he was bragging all the time. He didn't really come from a family of millionaires, but, just like I did at "Harry's" office back on Park Avenue, he was trying to brag about his wealthy family to impress people. He reacted immediately and we were yelling back and forth, getting more and more physically aggressive with each step in each other's direction.

The confrontation between us was broken up by "Mark" who nudged me along toward "The Dome's" entrance. We were all in the same TM class which was starting in five minutes, so we just continued barking back and forth while migrating inside.

And then I grabbed "Dave" and stabbed him in the face.

And then "Aaron", ironically, grabbed me from behind and restrained me.

Then I was forced to apologize to "Dave" in the hallway.

And now I was at "Stan's" apartment to cool off...

"I'm going to have to come home," I told *The Man* on the phone. "I messed up."

"Do it!" I heard him say, visualizing him nodding his head.

I looked over my shoulder to check on "Stan" in the living room. I was trying to keep an eye on him.

"Get the next plane home," *The Man* said.

Instead, I heard, "Honor the family. DO IT, DO IT, DO IT!!!"

After I hung up, I felt the sharp pain in my head again. I told "Stan." He sat me down to meditate. More humming and chanting. It didn't help. Now I was feeling worse.

"This should help," he said, walking into the kitchen area. He opened the fridge and pulled out a container of milk. Pouring some into a tall glass, he mixed the milk with a ground almond and sugar mixture and gave it to me. He said it was some kind of elixir. The cool drink tasted like the Marzipan I made back home, but it didn't make much of a difference.

Seeing I was still in pain, "Stan" suggested I get some sleep and offered me his bed to take a nap. Sleeping was a big part of meditation at the school and it was considered therapeutic. I tried to lie down, but I couldn't stop the sharp pangs in my head from attacking me. There was no "off-switch" to *The Genetic Microchip*, which was shooting sparks everywhere. I tried to close my eyes, but my mind was racing with rage.

Shubi S.

Turning over on my back, I laid there and stared at the ceiling. Deciding to tell "Stan" my dilemma, I got up and went back into the living room. He was gone. "Stan" had disappeared. I didn't know what had happened to him. Confused, I pulled back the living room curtain to see if "Stan's" car was still parked outside. It wasn't. I began pacing around the apartment theorizing about what was happening around the world and what was happening to my class action lawsuit - the lawsuit that would save the world from poverty...

The anticipation began rising inside my chest again. All semester I had been waiting for this big event to happen in my life. With "Stan" gone, maybe this was finally my time to shine. My head hurt so bad...

Suddenly I heard A*llah ... Allah ... Allah ... kill the Jew ...*

The words pulsated in my brain over and over again.....

Remembering my conversation with *The Man*, I logged onto "Stan's" computer to book myself a plane ticket home. Disoriented, I booked the wrong ticket for the right time, leaving *The Man* waiting for me, in vain, at the airport the next day.

The truth was, it didn't matter. It didn't matter because I wouldn't be home for the next seven years.

13

Point of No Return

I found myself back at "Stan's" living room window, people-watching. Maybe someone passing by on the street could give me some clues about what to do next. I kept asking myself: should I obey my father's message? "Do it, honor the family," he had said. *Do what?* My mind wanted to know. I needed clues, bad.

No one on the street looked my way or gave me any signs. Frustrated, I plopped down on the couch and turned on the TV. The world news was on. They talked about Africa. A tribal war was going on and the commentator stated that they would not put down their arms. I took that as a sign I needed to get armed.

Confused, I switched the channel. I wasn't sure if I should do what *The Microchip* was telling me to do … now, I was watching the Oprah Winfrey show. She was sitting on stage and the episode was coming to a close. When the camera zoomed in on her face she winked at me. Her wink told me to "go ahead". I thought, *if Oprah thinks I should do it, then it's GOT to be the right thing to do.* That was the clue I had been waiting for. I knew then what had to be done next.

After fumbling around in the kitchen for a few minutes, I came across what looked like a small steak knife with a wooden handle. I didn't know what I was looking for, but it seemed that the knife would suffice. All I knew was that I had to claim permanent damages to counteract the lawyers in the class-action lawsuit. They would have no choice but to award me the case once they saw how damaged I was by the devastating circumstances they had forced me into. Unsure of what my next move was going to be, I put the knife in my right pocket, got my jacket, and left.

I went outside, but had no clue where I was. The school seemed far away and I didn't know how to get there. I just kept putting one foot in front of the other. I don't remember how it happened, but I bumped into a lady. I hitched a ride with her. I thought she was designated to give me a ride. In my mind, she also knew who I was.

She talked throughout the entire ride, but I wasn't paying attention to her words. I was busy thinking about whether her giving me a ride was a good idea. If she assisted me in my mission I wouldn't win the lawsuit and save the world ... I didn't want her meddling to ruin the lawsuit.

"Drop me off NOW."

"You said the cafeteria, right?" she looked at me confused. "It's only a few minutes ahead."

"No, drop me off HERE." I was already tugging on the door handle. I don't think the car pulled to a complete stop before I was out and walking again. *The Microchip* wanted me to go to the cafeteria in the Student Center. I wasn't sure why, but I knew at that time of day people would be there. My head was pounding. Right before I entered the building I heard a name in my mind - I thought it was the name of my adversary...

When I went inside, there were tables occupied with some of my classmates who were talking, laughing and eating. I even saw "Stan" at one of the tables having lunch with the other faculty members. Everything appeared normal. I got some food and sat down at a table. Now, I was looking for Germans to give me a sign.

I spotted the half-German "Wesley" and took a seat at the table with him and two other German kids who were brothers. Considering what happened earlier that day, everyone was really nice to me. They didn't bring the matter up at all. I looked at the German brothers sitting across from me. They nodded. Obeying their signal, I switched tables and moved closer to the other students.

At my new table, a girl sat across from me - another German. A Jewish kid was seated to my right. His name was "Laurence". I'd seen him around and said hi to him a couple of times. He lived in my dorm. I even think we played video games together once. The German girl nodded at me and I knew what had to be done … I must kill the boy and save the world.

"Laurence" was a short, clean-cut kid eating his lunch. I asked him where he was from.

"California," he said, taking a bite of his sandwich.

California … I had been journaling a lot about the corporate conspiracy among the mega-media companies and many of them were located in places like California. Media=Hollywood. I thought about *The Radiologist* and how my brain was being scanned with radiation frequencies…

"Laurence" was eating an almond butter sandwich. The next thing I knew, my hand was in my jacket pocket and the knife was in my hand. I stood up and jabbed it in his back.

"What the fuck, man?"

I stabbed him again.

This time he didn't seem to resist.

I did it again.

It was just the two of us. The entire world faded to black in the background. It was just me and him - my oppressor.

I continued my attack with steely intent, showing the lawyers how their torment had affected me. They had pushed me over the edge and now I was going to turn the class-action lawsuit on its head...

I saw my oppressor's eyes - two blue eyes that were really sharp and clear like the ocean. His face was contorted into harsh angles, his mouth hanging open, gurgled sounds escaping from his throat. I was taller and more physically powerful than he was - a small guy and an elegant, good-looking person. He was cool ... but I had my orders. Still holding the sandwich, his hands were flailing and the almond butter got smudged onto my shirt. He couldn't break free. My arms felt stronger than I'd ever felt them, with a mind of their own - digging a tunnel into the earth with a spoon. Thirty seconds unraveled into a lifetime as I fought the enemy for liberation. I was taking my oppressor by surprise and, of course, he was shocked. Shock makes the eyes peel wide open and the pupils dilate. Those shocked, dilated blue eyes - eyes that will haunt me forever - locked into mine.

"WHAT THE HELL ARE YOU DOING?!" I heard "Stan's" voice from behind. Suddenly the blackness dissolved to an illuminated scene of screaming students and sheer pandemonium. I felt the salient pinch of "Stan" grabbing my arm. He seized the knife and twisted my arm behind my back.

By then, "Laurence" was clutching his chest, sliding down to the floor. People were screaming in terror as "Stan" muscled me outside. He demanded to know why I did what I did. I looked at his pale, German face, which was now beet red. His warm countenance had hardened into sheer fury. He looked like he was going to explode.

As he paced back and forth, swearing, clutching his head and rubbing his eyes underneath his glasses in shock and disbelief, I realized he could never understand my mission. I was trying to shut down the big lawsuit on behalf of the People. In the distance, the faint whining of sirens drew closer and closer. My resolve turned to emotional distress. I began to feel miserable about what I had done. And now the lawyers were coming for me.

The wailing sound turned out to be a cop car, bathing us in pulsating red and yellow lights. Behind it was an ambulance. By then, a crowd had started to form in front of the building. I glanced back at the entrance doors where faculty members and some of my classmates were huddled together, looking on. The paramedics jumped out and were greeted by the ex-Air Force pilot who got them up to speed and led them inside. The doors were held open as the medics rushed the stretcher through.

"Is this him?" The police officer was asking "Stan". In the movies, these were the moments where things moved in slow motion…

"Turn around."

My eyes rolled up to the sky as I was shoved against the hood of the car and my hands were locked together behind my back in tight metal cuffs. It hurt, but all I could do was wince and look to the heavens to help me. The clouds looked like big cotton balls floating on the crystal blue seas of the sky and the Midwestern sun showered the landscape with warm golden rays.

There was that blue again. First "Laurence's" eyes and then the sky. It was a painful irony. Some of the most beautiful weather I'd ever seen on the darkest day of my life.

The officer opened the door and stuffed me in the backseat. A few other cop cars arrived and the building became a crime scene. They were covering everything in yellow and black tape. I looked at the crowd,

Shubi S.

which was getting bigger by the minute. A news van had pulled up behind the ambulance and the crew was setting up. One of the officers was asking my classmates questions. I couldn't hear what he was asking them, but I could tell they were talking about me. It didn't matter what any of them said. No one could understand what I was dealing with. I had a class-action lawsuit to win. And I was raging against the beast - a beast which could take me out at any moment.

The two officers got in and rolled down the window to confirm a few things with "Stan". He never looked in the backseat the whole time I was there. He couldn't even look me in the eyes. There were no words to say like last time. But he was right about one thing: I had had a stressful day. Overwhelmed, I broke down into tears and couldn't stop.

"I did it. I win!" I kept repeating while sobbing uncontrollably. It was finally over. No more being chased by the lawyers working on behalf of the media and pharmaceutical companies. I hadn't asked for this mission. I hadn't wanted to carry it out. But now, I could be free. The world could be free.

14

I Don't Know Why the Caged Bird Sings

"You're being charged with first degree murder," the police officer said without looking up from his paperwork.

My face had no expression. I couldn't understand what murder he was talking about. I was responding in self defense, winning the lawsuit by claiming permanent damages. I was supposed to be free now. Instead, I found my wrist handcuffed to the officer's desk.

Things felt surreal and cloudy. In a police station, there was no sense of hours or minutes. White men wearing blue uniforms bustled back and forth. Some were shuffling paperwork, others were escorting prisoners in handcuffs and some were answering the phones, which were ringing loudly every few minutes.

I was allowed one phone call and I called *The Man*. His rant about me not showing up at the airport came to a halt when I told him I had been arrested. He couldn't imagine what I was about to tell him. I had called home with some bad news before, but nothing like this.

There was no need for an interrogation and no option for bail. My "self-defense" had taken place in front of about twenty people. It was a wrap. They took my fingerprints, processed me, and stuck me in a holding cell in the center of the police station. Feeling betrayed when I was supposed to be free, I paced feverishly back and forth in the cage like a panther. "GOD DESTROY THIS WORLD!!!!" I screamed over and over again. Some officers passed by holding coffee paused to shake their heads as I continued to scream and slam myself against the metal bars. Others ignored me. Some yelled at me to calm down. While a few asked the officer processing my paperwork what my deal was.

Night had fallen and my parents had to wait until the next day to fly out, so they moved me to the back of the building where the real jail cells were. It was definitely an upgrade, with a television and a small cot. The guard locked me in and I plopped down on the hard mattress. The TV was already on. Mega-church preacher, Creflo Dollar, was delivering one of his sermons. As he was strutting back and forth in front of the huge crowd, he had a special message just for me:

"*The mission is not complete.*"

Not complete? I felt my heart drop to the pit of my stomach. It had to be complete. I looked down at my shirt where the almond butter stain used to be before they took my clothes and gave me a prison uniform. After all I did - the hospitalizations, homelessness, constantly looking over my shoulder, moving halfway across the country to go to meditation school - and THEN stabbing "Dave" and "Laurence." It still wasn't over?!? No. I couldn't bear that. I couldn't be such a failure. I had to take matters into my own hands.

I banged my head against the wooden bench adjacent to my bed. The guard in the hall heard the noise, ran over to my cell and told me to cut it out.

No way. I slammed my head again - harder. The guard yelled at me again while fiddling with his keys trying to get the cell door open to stop me. It felt so good. The pressure building up inside my head was relieved by the impact.

Murder and Misunderstanding

After he came in and gave me a second warning, I decided a better idea would be to take my prison pants and hang myself. I quieted down until the guard was satisfied. As soon as he left, I slid my pants off and knotted the legs around the highest rung of the cell bars. Then I placed my neck inside the crotch loop as tight as I could. Once I had enough leverage, I dropped my body weight onto the floor. The pants pulled tightly against my throat, dislodging my Adam's Apple. Before I could get it over with, several guards rushed in and pinned me down.

The comic book scenes were changing fast again. Suddenly, I was back in the squad room strapped in a chair singing, "God loves the little children," with tears and snot running down my face. When I got tired of that, I moved into a rendition of a Red Hot Chili Peppers song.

Another scene change. Now I was on suicide watch. They moved me to a locked room with padded walls. One thing about jail is that there are no windows. I couldn't tell whether it was night or day. I felt 'punked' by my adversaries in the class-action lawsuit, which made me scream incessantly at whoever was on the other side of the door. After a while, my throat started to hurt and I crumbled to the floor, drained of energy, trying to catch my breath. It seemed like hours before I heard the sound of footsteps in the hallway outside my door again. It was probably the lawyers coming to gloat over my demise. I'd show them.

"IS THIS THE BEST YOU'VE GOT?!" I screamed at the top of my lungs. "BRING IT ON, YOU SONS A' BITCHES!!!!!"

In the midst of my ranting and raving, the door hatch slid open and there stood the guard with my parents. I wasn't sure if it was a-hallucination or reality.

"*Shut up!* *The Man* said, solidifying that it was definitely real. "Stay calm in here. Just be quiet and don't do anything stupid!"

Shubi S.

That voice. In the state I was in, his crackly words felt like cold water being splashed in my face. Ever since I was a boy, there was something about the way he spoke to me that ricocheted off the corners of my soul and struck fear into my heart. He and Mom told me to hold tight while they got me a lawyer. I didn't have to worry about the lawyer because they already knew that the person needed to be non-white, otherwise I wouldn't trust him or her. *The Man's* sternness triggered the little boy in me and I quieted down - this time for good.

After my parents left, two doctors arrived to look me over. One was a Philipino lady who prescribed Clozaril. Admittedly, once I began taking it, I calmed down and was better. But, just like before, I became a drooling marshmallow. I guess it was better than trying to kill myself and singing Black-Eyed Peas songs.

While Mom and Dad were out looking for attorneys, I got a visit from the public defender. I wasn't impressed. He was a disheveled-looking, middle-aged guy whose suit needed some serious ironing. We met in the interrogation room to discuss my case.

I was suspicious of him from the get-go. It was probably a set-up, but I had no choice but to indulge him. As he shuffled through the disorganized piles of paperwork he pulled out of his briefcase, it seemed to me as if there was not a lot of public defending going on - just him explaining to me what the prosecutor was deciding to do and how we should go along with it. When he spoke with my parents, *The Man* kept asking him if he and Mom could assist him, pay him, help in any way, but he kept brushing them off.

"No, no, it's okay," he kept saying. "We're just going for a plea bargain." It was obvious he wasn't too interested in helping me, and my parents became more determined to get me a real lawyer than ever.

A hearing was scheduled to decide whether I was going to jury-trial or to settle a plea agreement. After they escorted me to my seat to decide my fate, Dad touched my shoulder gently, but firmly. "Don't worry," he said in a low whisper, "we got somebody to help you, don't worry."

He was right. The judge called for intercession and went to his side chambers to take a call. I turned to my parents sitting right behind me in the front row.

"What's going on?"

"I don't know," Dad's face looked uncertain. "It will be alright, don't worry."

When the judge returned, he was in different spirits. Pounding the gavel, he said there would be a continuance so that I could be evaluated to determine whether or not I was competent to stand trial. My public defender lawyer looked surprised, as if he was just being let in on the news. If it had been up to him, I would have followed his lead right into a plea agreement. I turned to my parents who were visibly relieved. They told me to be strong and that it would be alright.

That was the day "Johnny Cochran" walked into my life.

Later that night - around ten o'clock - as I was sitting in purgatory at county jail awaiting my next court appearance, one of the guards came to my cell and told me to get up because I had a visitor. County jail was really bland - a freezing portal of hell made with tan cinderblocks. I was living in a cell, which felt like a meat locker and the guards weren't exactly looking to turn up the thermostat and get me some fluffy blankets or put a mint under my pillow.

At any rate, the guard took me to one of the rooms filled with hard grey tables and chairs. There, front and center, sat this extraordinary black man. He was older - maybe over fifty - with curly, salt-and-pepper hair and the most expensive suit I'd ever seen. Coolness seemed to just ooze out of his pores. He wore classy spectacles and had a notebook with him. The guard ushered me to the seat across from him and returned to the back of the room to wait. "Johnny's" eyes met mine. He didn't ask to be my lawyer; he TOLD me he would be representing me from now on. Actually, he said that he had DECIDED to take my case.

I followed his lead and answered his questions.

"Do you know where you are?" He flipped his notebook open.

"Pennsylvania," I told him.

"What do you eat here?" he asked, looking preoccupied with his writing.

"Lamb Curry."

"Your mother comes in and makes it for you?" he glanced up, adjusting his glasses.

"Uh-huh. It's really good."

More notebook scribbling. There were a few long moments of silence. I wanted to ask what he was writing, but I was afraid to. I was the one being held against my will.

"Do you have a car parked outside?" he folded his legs, leaning forward in his chair.

"Yeah," I paused and smiled, "A Mercedes Benz."

"Okay." A few minutes passed with him writing again. Then he stood up abruptly and gathered his things. "I'll be in touch."

After our interview, "Johnny" set up some evaluations for me. He hired a forensic psychiatrist, the best in that part of the country. From what I could tell, the guy had some serious clout. I was going to need it, being that the state doctor had already put me on Clozaril while I was waiting to be evaluated again.

Out went "Johnny," and in came the forensic psychiatrist, an older guy who smoked cigarettes and shared a smoke with me when the guards left us alone. I couldn't stop staring at the protruding moles atop his bald pale head as he spoke. I liked him. He was a really nice, compassionate guy. It was the same orientation as "Johnny":

"Why did you do what you did?"

I didn't know what to say. I didn't want to give away the conspiracy against me with the class action lawsuit.

"I don't know what you're talking about," I replied mundanely.

"Do you have a Benz parked outside?"

"Yeah," I answered matter-of-factly.

"Hmmm, okay." He nodded his head in contemplation. I noticed he didn't have a notebook like "Johnny". The guy must have had a good memory.

He declared me insane and I was shipped to "Oakwood" - a nearby state prison with a mental hospital ward. There, I met with the state doctor, a lady named "Dr. Greene," who wasn't exactly my biggest fan. In fact, she didn't believe I was mentally ill and wrote me up to go back to County for refusing to take my medicine. The suggestion that I was refusing my meds was ridiculous. In an earlier incident I had been instructed to go sit in a room where five or six guards swarmed me, pinning me down to the table. The next thing I felt was the burning pain of a long needle filled with Haldol being pumped into my shoulder. I was in shock. I would have taken it if they had asked me to. Why the guerilla tactics? After that, I'd been going out of my way to be docile.

"Dr. Greene" calling me competent was a problem, because that meant I should stand for a jury trial - a panel of people who would have gladly burned me at the stake. The prosecution was relying on her diagnosis to give them the green light to go after me. I was in a catch 22. She was writing me up as being non-compliant in taking my medicine, which wasn't true, but once the guards tackled me it legitimized her claim of my resistance. Once I began "willingly" taking the shots, I was labeled as being competent. So, I left "Oakwood" and was shipped back to County again.

Next, my second evaluation with the forensic psychiatrist. I was declared incompetent again, sending me back to "Oakwood" for mental treatment. "Dr. Greene's" expression said it all. She had failed her assignment and now become more determined than ever to label me competent - and make it stick this time.

The next move in the playbook was for the guards to say I was trying to escape. "Oakwood" was a maximum security prison with high barbed wire fences, towers with sniper-style armed guards, and a round-the-clock security watch. Not to mention I was on the Clozaril which had me so out of it, I barely knew who I was.

They put me in isolation for two weeks to punish me. This was a tactic to try to break me so that I would tell them what they wanted to hear - which was that I was faking and fully competent. The worst thing to do to someone with delusions is put them in a box and leave them there in deafening silence. When you're hearing voices, the demons are locked right in there with you. It's worse than any horror movie I've ever seen.

This box of horror was called the segregation unit. I found myself sitting there on the floor with *The Microchip*, pissed off and my mind racing. I would kill myself. No, I would just make them *think* I was going to kill myself. That would show them they were all wrong.

Instead, I earned myself an even worse room in the suicide smog with a hard mattress and no sheets. In prison the mentality becomes "tit for tat". Stated another way, you're going to make things hard for us, then we're going to make things hard for you. In the end, it hurt the prisoner more than the guards. I soon discovered that in my new surroundings.

It was a claustrophobic space with standing room for one. A barred steel door held a slot for food where the food tray was slid in. Along with the tray slot, the door had a small window laced with wires and a sliding hatch so the guards could look at me whenever they wanted. It was annoying, with the protocol being to check on me in 15 minute intervals. And squatting on the floor wasn't easy with the fire ants crawling on the ground in droves. The twin mattress was propped up on another cement section rising up from the floor. Any kind of box spring could be a potential weapon, so it was just the mattress. A steel, lidless toilet protruded from the other wall. (Toilet lids were lethal weapons, too).

There was no privacy or time alone to strategize. At the end of each interval, the guard checked my room for contraband to make sure I had no available resources to kill myself. Even sugar was considered a weapon of mass suicidal destruction. How someone could kill themselves with tiny packs of white sugar, I didn't know. All I knew was that I could only get one or two packs with each meal.

Food was the only activity that kept me going. As the days went by, the fifteen minute check-ups moved to twenty minutes and then to thirty minutes. After a while, it was down to every few hours. They were nice enough to let me have magazines to read, but I was unable to concentrate. So, I sat there hour after hour, waiting for the sound of footsteps in the concrete hallway, which meant the guard was on the way with my food. Sometimes I sat there on the floor in front of that slot for five hours straight, just waiting for my breakfast or lunch to arrive. When the guard finally slid the metal tray in, I knew for the next ten minutes my mind would be occupied and I wouldn't have to think about my problems. That little routine became my life for the next two weeks.

Luckily Mom and Dad were allowed to visit me. Visiting hours were in four-hour increments, but they scaled my parent's time down to two. We met in some kind of communal room for visitors. My parents sat there as the guards brought me in shackled and cuffed. The chains connected my feet to my hands and I had to slowly shuffle my way across the room to sit down. Words could not describe the humiliation I felt with my parents having to see me that way.

Once I sat down, the guard stood over me with his arms folded. Trying to pretend he wasn't there, Dad would attempt to encourage me:

"You don't need to escape, bud." he said. "We're going to get you out of this one."

"I wasn't trying to escape!" I replied in broken Hindi.

He understood, but played along for our unwelcome audience. "Yeah, yeah. But don't try to escape, okay?" We both locked eyes and silently acknowledged that the walls had ears in that place. Once again, his gentle kindness and loving arms were reaching out to pull me back from the edge. I was delusional, but I wasn't hallucinating what was happening to me. The state wanted to pile on another charge of willful intent with the accusation of me plotting to break out of prison, making me a permanent menace to society.

At the end of my two-week stay, "Dr. Greene" requested to see me. The guards took me upstairs and placed me in a room to talk with her. She looked cynical, as usual. I could see it in her eyes. She wanted to break me. And so did the deputy warden.

"So, why did you do what you did?"

Here we go again, "Did what?"

"You tried to escape. Mr. Sars told me that you were trying to escape." She gestured toward the deputy warden.

"What? I wasn't trying to escape"

"Yes you did," the deputy warden burst into the conversation, his voice escalating.

The rest of the meeting seemed to last forever, with the warden screaming at me non-stop and Dr. Greene pounding me with the same questions over and over. They wanted a confession.

"Why did you do it?!"

Mentally drained and desperate for an escape, I broke down and told them what they wanted to hear. I just wanted to go back to the other unit, where I had my roommates, a bigger room and more livable surroundings. I thought if I confessed they would send me back and take me out of isolation. That didn't happen until "Dr. Greene" filled out the paperwork and declared me competent one more time. Now, I was on my way back to County again.

It felt like forever until my trial. I was caught going between "Oakwood" and County jail with "Dr. Greene" and "Johnny Cochran's" doctors hitting my diagnosis back and forth over the net. They had me moving every couple of weeks or months. It was hard to keep track of time. I spent a lot of it watching TV, especially the Food Network. In the middle of Emeril shouting "Bam!" while throwing garlic into a frying pan for the thousandth time, I couldn't take it anymore. I asked for the guard so I could use my phone privileges.

I called "Johnny's" office to see how my case was going. He wasn't available, but I got a lady attorney who was a part of his legal team. This man had it all - a private jet, a huge lavish home, a swarm of legal staff to work on cases and a lifestyle most people only fantasize about. The lady lawyer said I shouldn't worry. They just wanted to make sure they did a good job on my case which was why it was taking so long. Even though she was really polite and answered my questions, I knew the real reason why I was sitting in jail all this time…

Politics. "Johnny" and his people understood the game. I had to stay in jail long enough to appease the public, so that they were not outraged. I knew they wanted to fry me for what I had done. As she was talking, I realized that people don't understand mental illness and how it is a sickness. People just wanted an eye for an eye and a tooth for a tooth. The trial was taking place in a small Midwestern community that was kept running by "The University". This meant my case was not good publicity for them or the town. I had a bad feeling about the situation. Letting me go too easily, if at all, would be bad PR for potential students and tourism.

The next court appearance I made was with my new savior "Johnny Cochran". He pled to the judge on my behalf, requesting I be allowed a bench trial instead of a jury trial due to my incompetency.

The judge agreed. He asked me, "Do you understand this?"

I said yes.

Then he said, "Now you understand that *blah blah blah*…"

I don't care, I thought. I'm just going along with whatever "Johnny" says.

"Yes," I answered.

15

The Jury is Out

At my bench trial, it was a packed house. There were cameras filming along with a loud buzz of conversation in the air. The guards escorted me to my seat in the front of the courtroom. "Johnny" had gotten me a suit and tie from the local Wal-Mart for my court appearance. It was a little snug with me putting on weight from the Clozaril, but it served its purpose. Wearing regular clothes made me feel normal - as normal as I could feel shackled, cuffed and on trial for murder. By this point I had realized just how heavy this thing was. In my delusional state, I had killed someone and now I could go to jail for the rest of my life and then some. Thankfully, the state I was being tried in didn't have the death penalty.

While "Johnny" and his assistants were setting up, I took a look around and observed the crowd. Most were strangers I had never seen before. Scanning the sea of white faces, I wondered if "The University" staff was there. It didn't look like it. I assumed since they were involved in this debacle they would want to show up. I admit, I felt a little angry given that they bore some responsiblity (in my opinion). When I stabbed the first guy in the cheek, no one called the police. They tried to keep things hush-hush. So where were they now? To piss me off more, "Johnny" reminded me that I was not allowed to say the secret word "icine" because it was patented by the school. That made me mad at the ex-Air Force pilot, too. And speaking of him, where was he? And where

Shubi S.

the hell was "Stan?" He knew I was unstable. Instead of getting me medical help, he left me alone in his apartment so he could go have lunch with his faculty buddies. I'm not trying to shift blame, but there were a number of University staff members who were negligent in their actions.

Mom and Dad were in the front row behind me. I felt stronger with them there. I also noticed that the priest was sitting in the back row. He was an old guy I'd met in County jail where the only religious practice was Catholicism. Every day I went to the small chapel for bible study. Anything was better than sitting in my cell staring at the walls. The guy was nice, but he wasn't pulling for me at all. He asked me what I was in jail for and I told him. His response, in so many words, was to take my punishment and spend the rest of my life behind bars. All that was important to him was that I avoid eternal damnation by accepting Jesus as my Lord and Savior. As I watched him sitting at the back of the courtroom, I could hear him saying I needed to be saved over and over and over again. It reminded me of the imam in Indonesia. Be saved, get circumcised. Even in my drug-induced stupor, I couldn't help wondering why, if Jesus was saving me, did the priest want me to go to prison for the rest of my life? Wouldn't this Jesus rescue me if he was going to make me a new creation? In my darkest hours I would cry out to God to help me, especially when I had mental breakdowns. What wasn't I getting here? And it seemed like everyone, from the priest to the imam to the ex Air-Force pilot, was more interested in saving my soul than helping me. As the judge walked in and we stood up to salute him, I decided that my only savior was "Johnny Cochran".

As the trial proceeded, I kept staring at all the books. There were stacks of them on the table in front of me, filled with evidence "Johnny" and his associates had compiled on my behalf. Some of the books were thick - more than a novel, similar to an encyclopedia. I couldn't make out the titles on the covers, but I guessed they were judicial books, all piled into boxes - all about me. This lawyer of mine wasn't playing.

"Johnny" submitted these boxes to the judge for evidence, one by one. He was sporting another expensive suit and wing-tipped shoes, looking sharper than ever. He didn't appear worried at all. Before we stood up to begin the trial ceremony, he whispered to me to stay cool, that he had it under control. As always, his voice was really calm and smooth as he spoke to the judge. It was fascinating to listen to the magical quality of his words.

I was sitting there helpless, unable to keep pace with the chain of events that was soon to decide my fate. The judge called the forensic psychiatrist to the stand. The old man strolled to the front of the courtroom, not breaking a sweat. It was obvious he was well respected there.

Meanwhile on the other side of the room, the defense looked white and plain, dressed in drab, budget suits with neutral colors. The prosecutor looked like he went suit-shopping at Wal-Mart, too. They seemed very intense and serious as they asked the psychiatrist questions. "Doc" was un-phased and had an answer for everything. I couldn't follow his words, but I knew he was explaining our sessions and my illness in detail.

After the psychiatrist gave his testimony on my behalf, "Johnny" did some kind of power-point presentation on what was happening inside my brain. He had also gotten a hold of the medical form I had filled out in "Dr. Smith's" office. This guy really did his homework. He said that I had tried to get help but was dismissed in various ways. He also read to the judge my interview with him while I was in County Jail to prove I was not in my right mind when he first came to see me.

Shubi S.

At the end of the day the judge pounded his gavel and left to deliberate. I don't remember exactly how long it took for him to come back with his decision, but it was about four or five days. Finally, we were called back to the courtroom and he made his entrance. He told me to stand up for the verdict. You could hear a pin drop. My hour of reckoning had come.

The judge gave his speech - *blah, blah, blah.* I felt like I was underwater, drowning in it all.

And then his verdict came down:

Not-guilty by reason of insanity.

I remember looking around for signs on people's faces to see if I was winning or losing. My parents, who were more in touch with reality than I was, hugged me joyfully and said to hang tight for just a little while longer. Mom was crying. Now I felt relieved. I won. It was over – finally, the class-action lawsuit was over.

16

Life on the Inside

The judge pounded his gavel once more and stood up to leave, his long black robe rustling softly. I looked on in slow motion as he navigated himself toward the open doorway behind the bench. Anxious, I spun around to see my parents. Mom grabbed my hand as one of the court officers grabbed my other arm. "What's going on?" I said, confused as he grabbed me. I was supposed to be going home. In a fleeting moment, I searched my parent's dark watery eyes for answers. What I saw scared me. "No, bud," *Dad* said gently, but firmly. "You have to go back with them. But don't worry - you'll be home soon." Our family moment was shattered by the guards cuffing me and pushing me out of the room.

I was put in a prison van and driven back to "Oakwood". "Oakwood" was a huge facility in a very rural Midwestern setting. Looking out of the van's caged windows at the rolling pastures was one of the longest trips of my life. I didn't understand why I was going to jail if I was declared not-guilty. Something was off and my stomach was in knots. I could sense impending doom.

We pulled into the garage and the armed officer transported me inside. In the lobby he had to remove his gun. Then they closed the door behind him (the ones that buzzed you in). Once he disarmed himself he was allowed to take me inside. I was brought into a room to strip down and put on the "Oakwood" gear - a solid, electric orange-colored suit. But first I had to be searched. This was no patting down your clothes at the airport – here, you had to be butt-naked. I found myself face to face with a huge dude with one glass eye who had to be six-foot-something. He told me to bend over and spread my butt cheeks to see if I was hiding anything in there. Whether I liked it or not, things were about to get VERY intimate.

He was bent over behind me with a flashlight like my asshole was a cave he was exploring.

I tried to stop myself, but I had both hands pulling my butt cheeks apart as wide as I could. I let one rip - right in his face. It was loud. I couldn't help it.

Now the guy was furious and extremely humiliated. "ARE YOU GOING TO APOLOGIZE FOR THAT? ARE YOU GOING TO APOLOGIZE?!!!!!!!" He screamed at me like I was a goof-off army cadet and he was the drill sergeant. "Uh, sorry," I mumbled, trying hard not to show how funny I thought it was. What did he expect to happen?

After he finished his search which included me lifting up my ball-sack to let him take a look - we were done. Luckily I was drugged up on the meds, so the impact of my manhood being compromised felt more like a bad dream than a nightmarish reality. I slid into a new "Oakwood" uniform and went to take fingerprints and a mug shot. Afterwards, I found myself sitting in an office doing an intake with a pencil-pusher behind a desk. The woman had a whole list of things to tell me:

"These are your belongings," she pointed to a plastic Ziploc bag laying on the desk with my stuff in it. "You have fifty bucks you are taking in with you. We will put that in your inmate account transferred over from the County D.A. Here are the rules. This is your picture ID. And here is your nametag." The next thing I received was a white nametag with my picture on it and instructions to write my name in the space provided. She took the photo ID back and slid a sheet of paper across the desk with a list of prison rules and regulations.

While I was doing that, there were tons of questions flying at me in a machine-gun-like manner:

Do you have AIDS?

Do you have tattoos?

Do you want to get tested for AIDS? Here, sign this consent form…

All protocol, I suppose. I just wanted to go home.

However, at the moment, home was "Oakwood's" West Side unit. The patients called it "Wess-sigheed!" as proclaimed in all the West-coast rap songs. It was a place for the criminally insane - people who had mental problems and had committed crimes on top of that. It was an all-guy-lockup unit with four inmates to each room and four flatbeds.

Next I met my new roommates. There was:

"Clarence" also known as "K-9". "Clarence" was a tall, black guy serving hard time for allegedly resisting a police officer who busted him selling crack. It was his third offense on the "three-strike" law.

"Carter" was a skinny, white guy in his twenties. He was on meth and looked like it, too. He was rough around the edges, but had a great sense of humor. I think he was in for either assault or murder.

"Charlie" was a short Chilean dude we called "E-wok" because he was hairy, short and round with a huge beard - just like the creatures in Star Wars. He was in for assault. Eventually he was transferred to a group home.

Shubi S.

To my relief, "Dr. Greene" was gone and I now had a wonderful Indian doctor who was very intelligent and compassionate. She placed me on a new medicine named *Abilify* - along with another drug which was a life-saver. My new "cocktail" had side effects, of course, but it was much better compared to what I was taking before. Overall, I suppose the situation could have been much worse.

Being together all day, every day in the same concrete jungle forces you to bond with people. Of course, "K-9" was the leader and we all mostly fell in line. He was a bit of a thug who was feared by most of the other inmates. But he was also a ladies' man who knew everybody. Female social workers would come in to do intakes and he'd be flirting away. "Check this out," he'd wink at me in preparation for the compliments he'd throw her way as she was walking out the door. Sometimes he'd serenade the female employees with love songs. He used to brag to us about all of the staff members he'd hooked up with, too. Who knew if any of it was true?

The first major enterprise that "K-9" led us into was a coffee-smuggling ring in the cafeteria. The inmates weren't allowed anything but decaf, so the demand was there. "K-9" had inside connections with some of the junior workers from the general population who agreed to smuggle small packets of caffeinated coffee grounds through the laundry in time for commissary. They would wash the clothes and bring up the folded prison jumpsuits with coffee "dime bags" stashed in the pockets or nestled inside the pillowcases and the bed sheets.

Commissary was a prison canteen store where we could buy stuff once a week. We could use our prison accounts to pay for what we wanted. As in the real world, what you could afford depended on how much you had in your account. We earned some money for the jobs that we worked and friends or family could deposit funds into them on our behalf.

At any rate, the scheme worked like this. The coffee station gave us empty Styrofoam cups to put our decaffeinated coffee grounds in. At *commissary*, the four of us would get the usual decaf. Then we would also buy the most expensive item on the menu - M&Ms. All they had were the regular ones in the brown packaging. We'd buy every single package - mainly funded by me and "Carter," since we had the most money in our accounts. Then we would take our candy and coffee cups either to the laundry room or the bathroom to make the switch. Out went the decaf in the sink and in came the newly-obtained caffeinated coffee grounds.

Our best-selling product was the "Yak". "Yaks" were special cocktails we created, a hot liquid combination of M&Ms mixed with the caffeinated coffee grounds. It would spin you out, but it was worth it – a temporary escape your rather shitty existence.

"K-9," forever being the salesman, thought it would be a good idea to sell the coffee grounds to other inmates to make a profit. He would be in the cafeteria wheeling and dealing. He wouldn't charge them at first – he'd give it away for free knowing they would come back for more. Mental patients who felt low most of the time loved the high of caffeine. That's when he began charging them a fee of cigarettes or tokens, since we weren't allowed to have money. I suppose this was a similar sales tactic "K-9" had used when he was dealing drugs on the streets.

Every day was the same:

6:30 A.M. - The guard would bang on our door and yell at us to get up. If you didn't move he would rip the covers off of you - rain or shine, sick or well, cold or hot, tired or awake. It didn't matter what time you went to sleep, you had to get the hell up. It was breakfast-time. Plus, you had to be out of the room so that they could go in and change the bed sheets and take the dirty clothes to the laundry.

Shubi S.

6:45 A.M. - The first thing we had to do was take our meds. We called it the "med-line". And that's just what it was - a line of drowsy patients/inmates waiting to get a little white cup of pills to swallow. We had to down the pills before the line could move forward.

7:00 A.M. - Time to go to the cafeteria to eat. I'd usually be dead-tired. And breakfast sucked. Every day it was the same cold sack: cereal, skim milk, a granola bar and two packets of punch - a generic type of sugary fruit powder "fortified with nutrients" and a cup of water to mix it in. No one liked the chalky powder except "Carter," so I always gave him mine.

8:00 A.M. - We'd be off to "fun" activities. It was go to the gym, play kickball for an hour or go to arts and crafts. Later, we'd have social workers who did other activities, like teaching us to make our own cookies or play board games, but most of the time we had to entertain ourselves.

The rest of the day was a repeat of the morning schedule with lunch, dinner, med-line, activity time, clean-up and bed-check with a few "once-a-week" things like *commissary* and visiting hours thrown in. Over and over and over again.

The staff treated us like we were sub-human, talking to us as if we were disobedient dogs. I realize we were all there for a reason, but we were still human. "Bubba" was the only security guard who was kind to us and acted as if we were part of the same species. A short, chubby, bald guy, he hobbled around cheerfully every day. I always looked forward to his shift. When he was on nights, he set up card games for us to play. The first game he taught us was called "Huckabucks"- a five-card game with a winning threshold of 15 points. Every hand won counted for 1 point. If you were set back a hand you lost 5 points. If you were bidding, you had to win 2 hands. We would sit there for hours, struggling to get

Murder and Misunderstanding

to 15. It was a bonding time where we sang songs and told jokes. I guess it was a lot like Dad and his fellow soldiers when he was in the Army.

Music helped us a lot. We were allowed to have a tape recorder and order music tapes from "Oakwood's" library. We ordered anything and everything - from Bob Seeger to R. Kelly and T.I. "Carter" went crazy over his new exposure to rap music. "Rubber-band man over the Taliban!" he was always screaming over the beat. It was funny seeing this short, skinny, white guy yelling rap lyrics instead of lyrics from his favorite group - AC/DC.

"K-9" sang a lot. He had a great voice. He sang while we played cards, when we cleaned up, while we took our showers in the morning and while we were in bed at night. His velvety voice echoed off the concrete walls in the darkness and earned him some threats from irritated roommates. I didn't mind. What did we need to go to sleep for anyway? Tomorrow was just going to be another today - a day with no meaning.

"Harlan" moved in after "Ewok" left for the group home. He was a small, black guy who was really nice. He seemed somewhat effeminate - one of those sassy types that said whatever was on his mind and made no apologies. I witnessed him stand up to "K-9" who saw his effeminate nature and tried to bully him. Watching "Harlan" get aggressive with "K-9" was really interesting, especially being that "Harlan" was puny compared to "K-9's" huge, muscular frame.

What "Harlan" lacked in muscle, he made up for with street smarts and confidence. A lot of stuff he talked about was not stuff I knew about, so I always had a lot of questions for him. If he told me to pass him a pack of smokes I wanted to know why he called them "menthols". I always had something to ask him. After a while he started calling me "Charlie Brown" because I had so many questions all the time.

Underneath his annoyance with me and his daunting sarcasm, "Harlan" had a big heart. During our down moments he'd drop little gems of wisdom on me. While playing card games he'd hip me to the game on the inside. "Watch out in here, Charlie Brown," he'd tell me, shuffling the deck with a cigarette dangling out of the corner of his mouth. "Keep yo ass out the stalls after seven. Stick wit us." Seeing my innocence, he told me things about prison life and how to stay alive (and keep from having to bend over and grab my ankles). He was also a singer and would sing almost as much as "K-9". Music was something that kept us feeling alive in that graveyard of a prison. Music was big.

There were fights all the time. "Harlan" was right. With no cameras in the bathrooms, a lot of fights took place there - especially between the guards' shifts. You didn't want to get jumped in the bathroom without guards to break it up. Inmates would also go at it in the rec room - the prison's communal area. With only one television set, inmates were always fighting over the channels. One person wanted this channel and another wanted that channel. So it became an issue. What channel we wanted to watch was one of the very few choices we had in a world where you had no control over your existence, so the level of frustration was constant.

No matter how hard I tried to avoid trouble, trouble always seemed to find me. There was this big, black guy who picked on me day after day. He kept calling me "dot- head" and would not leave me alone. He also had severe mental health challenges. One time, I was minding my business, watching TV when he confronted me. He was convinced I was saying mean things about him behind his back. The next thing I knew, a huge fist was swinging around the back of my chair with the goal of landing on my face. Startled, bleeding and doped up on meds, I somehow managed to stagger out of my seat and take a defensive swing at him. This guy was much bigger and stronger than I was, but I did it anyway. I wasn't about to bitch out in that chair and just take it. This was state prison and being a punk - like "Harlan" always told me - was like signing your own death warrant.

The next thing I knew, we were being pulled apart and I was sitting in what was called "the hole". This was solitary confinement used to punish us when we broke the rules. But "Oakwood" had no sense of justice. It didn't matter whether or not you were justified. It didn't matter who started the fight. In the state penitentiary there were no victims, everybody was going down. My nose was bleeding and pulsating in painful throbs when the paramedic came in and asked me if it was broken. I said no without thinking about it. He didn't bother to check it, he just left, locking me in once again. I sat there to rot with the oozing blood drying on my face. The time I spent in that hole was lonely, miserable and isolated. Not so unlike having an untreated mental illness. Sometimes I felt as if I had spent my whole life sitting in a hole. But even worse, I feared that I would never get out.

Luckily, these instances were few and far between because I had "K-9" watching my back. No one really messed with me when he was around. One time, this big, lanky white dude confronted me. The minute he opened his mouth, I knew where things were going.

"So, you're Hindu, huh?"

"Yeah," I answered, feeling nervous. I was in white, Christian country and this guy was a redneck-type.

He made another comment and my juices got flowing. I forgot that I couldn't fight.

"Damn right I'm Hindu!" I squared my shoulders and puffed my chest out. I inched closer to the guy, who was cracking his knuckles, ready for a throw down. Suddenly he backed up and walked away. Gassed up, I went back to my room, amped and shouting "I'm the man!" over and over again.

Shubi S.

"K-9" was shaking his head in amusement. "You're looking at the man. I was right behind you."

My bubble burst. But, seeing that he was the toughest dude in the *West Side* and that no one would mess with him, it was good to have him as an ally. Oh well, at least I stood my ground.

Chores were big. We had to perform certain tasks every day. It didn't matter that some of us were insane and others were dysfunctional. These menial tasks were mandatory. If we didn't do them, we were punished. They would strip away our freedoms, like going out to the yard or to the gym. One common punishment was having our soda pop privileges revoked. At night, we could get soda pop out of the hallway vending machine right before bed. We weren't allowed to have cash, so we were given tokens. If we didn't do our chores then we were denied our soda pop token. On those nights, I went to bed depressed.

That was all we did ... clean. They didn't even have janitors, because WE were the janitors. I was elected to be chief cleaning officer, which meant I was responsible for making sure the work got done on my unit - cleaning the toilets, showers, windows, making sure the beds were made, everything. Cleaning took place two hours a day - one hour in the morning and another hour after supper. I had to gather the guys together to wipe the tables clean once we were done eating.

It was a struggle trying to get the guys I was responsible for to do their chores. With a whopping salary of a buck ten a day, they weren't exactly motivated. Plus, the money didn't even go into our hands - it went into our inmate accounts for commissary purposes. And many of them didn't have much to hope for anyway. They were in jail, labeled mentally ill criminals. And with society and families that had giving up on them, they had no real future. A dollar and some cents wasn't going to change that. I guessed it was some type of escrow where they were collecting interest on our wages. Still, I was working hard. The more productive one was, the more they increased one's pay. And the more they increased my pay, the more M&Ms I could buy for "Yaks". Every two weeks there was a pay increase for those of us conscious enough to give a damn. My pay got up to a buck forty five a day.

The food was shit. Most of it was heavy, simple carbohydrates. Every time I turned around they were giving us dessert - especially the spongy stuff like angel food cake. It was like chewing a sugary dish sponge. We also were forced to eat a lot of butternut squash. The prison was in farm country and the local community had squash as the main crop. I tried to get creative by putting syrup on it, salt and pepper and whatever else I could doctor it up with, but squash was on my tray every day of the week. I ran out of ideas. Between the bad food, depression, and medication side-effects, I gained a lot of weight.

If we were really on good behavior, we'd get to go to the "West Side's" newspaper club. The club was run by this guy named "Peter", the activities director. He'd bring in 15 newspapers for us to read. He began each meeting by picking out an article and then going around the room asking each of us to summarize the article. When we tried to explain what we read, he bit our heads off and started insulting us. Jail wasn't the best environment for intellectual stimulation, but apparently "Peter" hadn't gotten that memo. With every member of the group doped up on meds and incarcerated, he should have guessed he wasn't speaking to a room full of academic scholars. No matter what answers we gave to his questions, it pissed him off. He was a very nitpicky guy. If the newspapers weren't folded back *just* the way he wanted, "Peter" would go ballistic and scream our heads off. Everyone hated his guts. Some inmates would stand up to his bullying and call him an asshole to his face. That was when he'd go to the guards standing outside the door and demand the guy be handled. Automatically, the rebels would be punished and sent to the hole.

Shubi S.

Most of our recreational time was spent playing card games. Besides "Huckabuck," we also played a lot of Spades and Hearts. (A lot of the guys played Dominoes, too, but I wasn't really into it). A roundtable of mentally ill card players was always interesting. Things would sometimes get out of hand and guy's feelings would get hurt. It didn't matter, though, because it was all we had to keep us occupied from the nightmare of our world. With my status being "not guilty by reason of insanity" I kept wondering when I was going home.

After two years at "Oakwood" things were heating up in the legal arena. "Johnny" had requested I be moved to a place more suited for mentally ill people. State prison was rough and dangerous for a mellow guy like me. It wasn't a place where you could afford to be doped up on meds and at a disadvantage. The judge agreed and signed the letter authorizing me to be transferred to the nearby State Mental Institution, but the Institution was resisting. Now, "Johnny Cochran" and his associates were at war with the State.

I found myself going back and forth to court for proceedings about my transfer. Usually, we would meet in a small room, one that was a lot more intimate than the courtroom I'd had my bench trial in. It would be me, "Johnny" and his assistants, the attorney general, the DHS (Department of Health Services), my parents and my social worker from "Oakwood". Also, testifying on the Institution's behalf, there would be a guy in a suit. He was the psychologist and it was obvious how hard he was fighting to keep me out of The Institution. Every court appearance came with another excuse for me to stay at "Oakwood". Either there weren't any beds available or he'd claim that I was potentially dangerous in a place where there were women and children as patients. For one of these meetings, my cousin, Chinku, now a grown, working man, wrote a long letter on my behalf to the court, testifying to my character. As the letter was being read aloud to the judge, I felt really fortunate to have such a wonderful, supportive family behind me.

At the end of a long month of court battling, "Johnny" called me at "Oakwood" and gave me the news. I was being shipped to "The Mental Institute".

17

T.M.I.

My stay at The Mental Institute lasted three years.

After my time at the state penitentiary, I figured I had to be moving to heaven. Heaven turned out to be another concrete campus in a small Midwestern town smack in the middle of nowhere. I was taken there in another cop car. The intake process wasn't as severe as "Oakwood" and I was thankful for that. They took me upstairs and made me take a seat in the hallway. It was a soft comfy seat, too. Heaven? Maybe not. But better than "Oakwood" for sure. Then…

"YOU GONNA BE MY FRIEND? YA WANNA BLOW JOB?!?"

Startled, I turned to see the source of the loud, child-like voice. Sitting next to me, I saw what looked like a forty-year-old, white man who had been forced into a dryer which had been set on high. He was wearing a white bicycle helmet with the strap buckled under his tiny chin. The miniature man continued firing crazy questions my way and it freaked me out. I jumped up and ran down the hall to the pay phone so I could dial "Johnny's" 1-800 number. The miniature man followed me to the phone and continued asking me questions.

"Johnny's" secretary heard the panic in my voice and quickly got him on the phone.

"This place is crazy! I want out! You gotta get me outta here!" I was almost screaming into the receiver. The little man's questions were getting louder and louder by the minute.

As always, "Johnny's" voice was smooth and calm as he told me to be patient. I tried to calm down and believe his words, but it was hard to do sitting on a wooden bench in front of a pay phone with this little guy in my face saying loud random things that made no sense. None of the workers passing by batted an eye to my terror.

Despite the psychologist's testimony in court about TMI's lack of available space, I noticed that there were empty beds in some of the rooms as they led me upstairs to my new living quarters. After I settled in and did all of the intake stuff, I was able to go into the main room with the television. When I walked into the communal area, a big smile spread across my face. Sitting at one of the tables playing cards were two of my old "Oakwood" associates: "Wayne" and "Carter". "Wayne" and I didn't get along that well. He was always irritable. On the contrary, I was excited to see my old roomie "Carter" again. He was declared incompetent to stand trial for murder and was transferred to TMI several months before. It was a nice reunion. In prison you never know what happens to guys when they leave with the guards. Seeing someone I was friends with in this new place where I knew no one was really comforting. "Carter" had gained a lot of weight since I last saw him. Being a former meth addict, he was skinny as a rail, but now he was chubby like me. As usual, he was all smiles and full of jokes.

I also ran into the psychologist from the transfer hearings. He was much nicer than before. In fact, we quickly became good comrades. We talked about the court situation. I wanted to know what his deal was and why he was fighting so passionately to keep me from coming in. He told me it wasn't him - it was just "business". In other words, he was following his marching orders.

Shubi S.

In the adult, male ward there was fighting on a daily basis. Just like at "Oakwood," what TV channel to watch was a major reason to go to war. It wasn't long before the bickering became a nuisance. Most of the patients weren't violent, but there were a few. I learned quickly not to judge a book by its cover, though. For example, the guy I'd met on my first day who had scared me, one of the nurses told me that he had a condition which made him unaware of what he was doing. And as I'll discuss later, he became an important part of my time at TMI.

There were more freedoms than at "Oakwood", but the sadness was ever-present. It was a roller-coaster of great highs and extreme lows, taking you from soaring above the clouds all the way down through the muck and mire of the gutter. I was one of the more fortunate patients because I had a family who cared back home that came to visit me regularly. They also sent me care packages. Many of the guys there had no support system and no hope, so they just lived for the moment and, with nothing to lose, nothing was out of bounds.

Every morning the staff would wake us up really early. As a rule, we were not allowed to go back to our rooms, so once we were up, we were up. Drugged, and extremely fatigued, we'd just camp out on the chairs in the common areas and try to rest. The chairs were hard, cheap plastic, so I laid down on the cold, ceramic floor sometimes and continued to sleep until a staff member yelled for me to get up. Every day there were "the codes" to deal with, too. Code Blue meant someone was having a heart attack or had stopped breathing and the doctor needed to come resuscitate them. Code Green (the most popular) meant a call for security to resolve fights between patients or between patients and staff members. And Code Red, which you never wanted to hear, meant that there was a fire.

What was really interesting about me being in a mental institution was the acceptance and popularity. Inside those walls I was respected more and people recognized that I was a good person who had a disease. Whereas, on the outside, I was viewed as nothing more than a treacherous murderer unwilling to take responsibility for my transgressions.

As for the staff, it was a mix of good and bad. Some were daytime, part-time staff. They tended to be the younger crowd and were usually nicer, but some of the resident staff members were the worst. They would break you down. It was an atmosphere of walking on eggshells. The slightest little thing and it would go into your chart. If I had a mood swing for five minutes, it was recorded in black and white. Because of this, I was very cautious to the point of paranoia. The resident staff kept telling me that if I did anything stupid I would get sent back to "Oakwood". So I made sure that I walked the fine line.

Not that prison is super clean, but at "The Mental Institute" things were a lot less sanitary. The communal bathrooms had curtains instead of doors, so the place stunk to high heaven. It was a crowded environment, making it hard not to transmit germs and disease. They would quarantine the sick person, but it was usually too late after being in close contact with everyone.

I began getting chronic bouts of the flu. Sitting there congested and drugged, I would feel like I was in a mentally ill version of *Thriller*. Guys would be staggering around like zombies, slowly dragging their feet, moaning unintelligible sounds from the dark belly of their tortured souls with distorted faces drained of all signs of life. Some of them didn't have complete control of their bowels, so they would have accidents. With their clothes soiled with feces, they'd keep walking as if nothing had happened. When they sat down on a chair, chances were good it was going to be smudged. Sometimes they peed on themselves. It was a sad environment. Not one in which any human being should have to live.

There were extracurricular activities to do at TMI. Of course, in order to participate you had to be on good behavior. Being on good behavior came with perks. The staff was much nicer to the "GB"s. They joked around with us and were much more laid back. Sometimes they even took us to get "pops" (soda), but stopped once the higher-ups found out. One of the male staff members used to bring us chew (chewing tobacco) and energy drinks, which was also against the rules. Some of the other recreation staff hooked us up, too.

One of my favorite perks was the ceramics class. I made all sorts of pieces and mailed them out to my family. Everyone loved my artwork. The art class was probably the most rewarding part of my stay there. Much as it had for my dad and grandfather in India, art allowed me to give back to people and express myself creatively.

And, since I was dotting my I's and crossing my T's, they also allowed me to be a part of the activities group. Everybody wanted to be in the activities group. The group leader was a fat, jolly pastor who had a church downtown. He would take us to the gym to play softball and to bible study once a week. He was really nice and good-humored. Sometimes he took us on a field trip to his church for Sunday morning services.

When word of my new extracurricular activities and outside trips got back to the prosecution's office, shit really hit the fan. They argued that since I was declared insane by the judge (not guilty by reason of insanity) that I was a danger to society and should not be allowed to leave the grounds of "the Mental Institute"- even if I was being chaperoned. "Johnny Cochran" stepped in and fought for me to be able to move up the ladder - so to speak - in order to obtain more privileges and freedoms. It was a long wait. And though I don't know how he managed it, "Johnny Cochran" once again came through and I was allowed to participate again.

My new status introduced me to a whole new world. I was now taking field trips once a month to the movies. A theater downtown

Murder and Misunderstanding

donated a bunch of tickets and the staff would pack us into buses and take us to see the latest flick.

Then, one day, the roller coaster ride took another twist and I got a new roommate - the guy who was freaking me out in the hallway my first day there. His name was "Gerry". The nurse helping him move in gave me the scoop: "Gerry" was in his forties, but was a child trapped inside a miniature, mentally retarded man's body. He was one of those unusual cases. Over twenty years prior, he'd been arrested for shoplifting in a candy store. He didn't have family - at least family who cared - so he got tangled up in the legal system where he was declared incompetent and sent to jail. He ended up at "the Mental Institute" after years of floating through the system. This was his last stop. At his age, all his family members were dead and he needed round-the-clock care. He was always walking too fast and didn't have the balance to hold himself up, so he was constantly stumbling and falling down - which was why he was wearing the bicycle helmet when I met him.

First impressions can be deceiving. "Gerry" turned out to be an amazing human being. He really helped me survive those next three years. He listened to me and I listened to him. We respected and loved each other, the type of love you get between two people who are alone and misunderstood in the world. "Gerry" gave me a reason to get up in the morning. Now someone else needed me. I wasn't stupid and incompetent anymore. I could help "Gerry" survive and take care of him. I was in bad shape myself, but his condition gave me something to be thankful for. Even though I was better off, I felt like I could relate to him. He understood about being an outcast. After what I had done, society would never be able to accept me the same way as before. Now, I wasn't so alone.

"Gerry" looked like a little boy - short, bald, except for a patch of hair protruding from the top of his head. One would think he was seven or eight years old. In actuality he was in his forties with no family to take care of him. So, he became a part of my family. When my mother came to see me, he'd call her by her first name and go climb in her lap. She always brought something for him.

Sometimes people treated him like he was stupid because of his child-like nature. The truth was that he was stuck in that hostile environment for years and a lot of his behaviors were defense mechanisms. The staff loved him, though. After becoming roomies, at dinnertime, I started to save him a seat in the cafeteria, but he'd be nowhere to be found. After it happened a couple of times, I went looking for him and found him in the kitchen with the staff getting his grub on. Apparently this was the usual routine for him.

He had the mind of a five year old child. When I took a shower, he would try to find me. I'd be soaping up and hear his voice echoing through the halls, calling my name:

"O-obiiiieee!! Where are you? Oobie?" (he called me *Oobie*). I would answer him and he'd follow my voice into the bathroom and pull back the shower curtain while I was in there.

"What you doin' Oobie?" he'd say, grinning.

"Dude, I'm taking a shower."

Then he'd proceed to talk to me as if I wasn't naked and covered with soap. He was a funny little guy. Every day was a continuous episode of the Bill Cosby show "Kids Say the Darndest Things". Now it was "Gerry says the darndest things." You never knew what was going to come flying out of his mouth. One time, I was playing around, dancing, trying to entertain him. He said:

"You can't dance. You're not BLACK. You not Mik-al Jack-son!"

During one of our usual shower run-ins, he looked at my flabby frame and said "Oobie, Oobie, you gotta get some muscles, Oobie."

I said, "Why "Gerry?"

"Because you can beat people up!" After I got out of the shower, he proceeded to coach me and help me do push-ups. A very funny little guy, indeed.

He also had some weird tendencies at times. Rumor among the staff was that he had been molested early on in his life. We'd be sitting there in our room and he would try to touch my penis, like a curious child. I would push his hand away and explain that he shouldn't do this.

There were other situations where his sexual abuse was evident. One of the inmates would be looking at him and he'd fire back, "YOU WANNA BLOW JOB?" What he really meant to say was, "Do you want to be friends?" But, he didn't know how to express himself. I would be a little strict with him sometimes. I figured he didn't know any better and no one had taught him otherwise. So, every time he'd say or do something inappropriate I'd put him on "time out" in a chair. I hoped if I did it enough times he would get a sense that he shouldn't do those kinds of things again. Right or wrong, I was genuinely trying to help him. Of course, there was an up-side to "Gerry's" child-like nature. He could get away with things no one else would even think about trying. When the nurse was helping him, he would thrust his head inside her cleavage and nuzzle his nose in her breasts. The nurse, familiar with his crazy antics, would just wag her finger at him.

Every now and again I would get a meeting with the in-house psychiatrist. He was supposed to show up every week, but he had a long list of TMI patients to handle all by himself. Besides, we weren't worthy of too much effort in the eyes of these people. As far as they were concerned, if we were in bad enough shape to get admitted there, then no amount of sessions was going to help. When we did meet, our sessions were focused on me being "under control". All he was there to do was to make sure I was taking my medicine and that it was keeping me in line.

Shubi S.

Sometimes we'd talk about what happened, but "the incident" was somewhat of a trigger. At first mention of it, I would disassociate myself. With the stress of pleasing *The Man* no longer an issue, my suspicious thoughts were dissipating. I felt myself beginning to feel my true emotions, which put me more in touch with reality - and the pain - again. The drugs were diffusing *The Genetic Microchip* and I wasn't feeling the sparks in my head anymore. The reality of my grandiose delusions was hard to come to terms with. It was like falling from a mountain peak into a valley.

I remember those sea-blue eyes. I hurt for his family. People think I don't care. I do. But, at the time, it was difficult with a doctor and staff writing down every word and deed on paper for documentation - either supporting or denying my "not-guilty by reason of insanity" status. I was only the second case won under that verdict in the state. And I was one of the youngest to receive it anywhere. If I opened up about my realization with the murder, people would assume I was faking and that I had intentionally killed "Laurence". It's hard to describe, but the last few years were like sitting in the backseat and watching someone else drive the car I called my body. I had cognitive dissonance, where one side of me was paranoid and the other side was being held hostage.

In the meantime, my new hobby became going to the library. I never used to read many books, but with so much time on my hands my brain was slowly turning to mush. While perusing the shelves, I came across a used paperback named "The World is Flat" by Thomas Friedman. It was an amazing, simple read that spoke many truths to me. Reading about the outside world made me feel normal again. Another thing that made me feel good was going to the library's CD player and listening to music. Music was my getaway. I was also going on a lot of field trips (after "Johnny" got me cleared) to places like museums. One particular museum was full of old cars. Another was full of old trains. We went to a fishery, too - all kinds of interesting places.

The staff, for the most part, was numb to our plight of mental illness. This was a small town, so the hospital was its bread and butter. That being the case, the turnover rate was very low for TMI employees. Some knew we needed help. Many were very apathetic. They didn't consider us to be human. I'd knock on the door to the staff office and they would take forever to open it. In fact, the door was all glass and I could see that they purposely ignored me as if I didn't exist. Sometimes, they would be sitting right in front of me having a casual conversation and would act as if I was invisible. Apathy is worse than outright cruelty - especially to someone mentally ill. Small things affect how people behave. Treat individuals, mentally ill or not, with kindness and respect and you will get a better reaction.

Despite my friendship with "Gerry," I started feeling restless. I wasn't the normal everyday inmate. Many of the patients there had mild to severe intellectual disabilities. I had a family who cared about me and I had traveled the world. I also went to college, so that put me ahead of the pack. Looking for something to do, I went to the main office to talk to the woman in charge of patient activities. I asked her if I could take classes. The local community college had what were called correspondence courses - the precursor to online courses today. She said okay and registered me for one class. I was glad to finally have something constructive to do.

We used to take a lot of chaperoned walks on the campus. We walked around looking at the big brick buildings, many that had been built during the civil war. These structures were old-school, not made with the thin plaster of today. The summer meant the heat was trapped inside and the winter meant the cold would be trapped inside - at least that was what one of the staff members told me. During those walks, I learned lots of stories about the way they treated mentally ill patients back in the day - electric shock therapy, lobotomies … Though the treatment I was receiving was less than ideal, I was thankful I wasn't around back then.

Shubi S.

My family became regulars at TMI. Mom used to come every other week to visit me - quite the expensive proposition, flying in from the east coast. Sometimes my sister would come with her, along with one or two of my cousins. After some time on good behavior, I also earned visitor's privileges which allowed me to take my family on a tour of the campus by myself.

Dad flew in with Mom and sis to see me, too - on occasion. He had his businesses to manage and "Johnny's" bills to pay - on top of my defaulted student loans from "The University". Oddly, he became friends with "Jason"- one of my fellow inmates. "Jason" was a lifer at TMI just like "Gerry". During my family visits, "Jason" would come around and he and Dad would talk basketball and other "buddy" topics. I kept reminding Dad that the guy had a mental illness and was not well at that point. Dad's friendship with him extended to the point where the kid had our home number. Sometimes he would call Dad to talk. Having someone to talk to is really important, but this was not a good situation, since their interactions made "Jason" believe he was an eligible candidate to be Dad's future son-in-law.

Every time they were in town, "Jason" would ask me about marrying my sister. It all started when he helped protect me from one of the more violent guys on our floor. The next morning, in the bathroom, he approached me while I was brushing my teeth.

"I save your life one more time, Shubi, and I get to marry your sister."

I halfway smirked and bent down to spit out my toothpaste froth into the sink, which made him angrier. He kept repeating himself over and over again. Annoyed, I said no and told him to leave me alone. In a momentary strike of superhuman fury, he cracked the sink he was standing in front of, took one of the porcelain shards and held it to my throat, repeating his request:

"If I save your ass one more time ... I-GET-TO-MARRY-YOUR-SISTER!!!"

Thank God for round-the-clock surveillance and Code Green. Still, for some reason, Dad liked him - probably because "Jason" had no one on the outside that cared for him - at least not enough to come see him. *The Undercover Sialkot Indian Artist* felt empathy for him, so the least Dad could do was give him some conversation.

One of the staff members my family grew to love was a gay man who made quilts in his spare time. He brought his works-in-progress to the job so he could finish them during his lunch break. I was fascinated by the sight of him sitting there in the corner, kneading away. He allowed me to sit with him and let me ask questions. I ended up getting a piece of one quilt, another one for my sister and another for my mom during one of their visits. His work was beautiful and varied. One had a Native American sun dial filled with shades of orange and blue, a real stunning piece. Another quilt was decorated with abstract designs of rectangles and squares. He gave that one to my sister.

Another family-favorite employee was the "Jiu-Jitsu Specialist". "The Specialist" was a world-renowned *Jiu-Jitsu* competitor who had finished third in the world and was a state champion. *Jiu-Jitsu* is a type of martial art. An avid athlete, "The Specialist" was fit and in shape, making him perfect for the job. Whenever there was a "Code Green" in one of the wards (which happened several times a day) his karate skills came in handy as he rushed over to restrain whoever was acting out. He had his own studio, but TMI was the gig that paid the bills. During his personal time, he took troubled kids from his neighborhood and got them involved in the studio learning martial arts. With all the overhead costs like uniforms and equipment, he was just breaking even at the end of the day. There truly are some amazing people in this world.

Shubi S.

"The Specialist" and I became fast friends. At night, after everyone went to bed, he and I sat together shooting the breeze with the other staff members in my dormitory unit. I lived in what was called "the B side", the section of the building where the adult male inmates stayed. After hours, when patients went to bed and the pace of things slowed down, the staff congregated in the back of the cafeteria to take a cigarette break, eat and socialize with each other. Unable to sleep from the caffeinated drinks the daytime staff slipped me "under the table," I would often join them.

"The Specialist" would tell me stories of winning his tournaments and travelling the world. I listened to all of his amazing experiences. He was a "Christian Buddhist"- as he liked to put it- and we spent hours having dialogue about religion and different belief systems. Sometimes, one of the other staff members would join in and it would turn into a roundtable discussion. We kicked philosophy, talked about girls, movies … we had a lot of fun conversations. A savvy bachelor, "The Specialist" was well skilled in the kitchen. Every night there was a new dish he had whipped up and brought in for lunch. One of his favorite things to make was a vegetable stir-fry with pan-fried steak strips. Knowing how awful the food was at TMI, he made it a habit to bring extra for me and "Gerry". I did ask him to bring me caffeinated drinks too, but he refused to sneak me any of those. He had to draw the line somewhere.

We spent many a night in the "B side" talking about "Gerry" and how awesome he was and how he was positively changing our lives. One time "The Specialist" said, "I don't really love any girl, but I love 'Gerry'". This guy was a bona fide ladies' man, but when it came to the purest form of unconditional love there was none that stood out, but the affection he had for this little guy. Like so many others, he just loved "Gerry". Sometimes he sat there writing in his journal about "Gerry's" non-stop antics, which was always a new topic for conversation.

I totally shared "The Specialist's" sentiment. In the darkest hours of my illness, I discovered the most beautiful light. "Gerry" showed me how to be a parent. You don't know love until you're completely responsible for someone else and you care for them unconditionally. That kind of love was something I had been looking for all my life. It was always there, but I didn't truly experience it until I gave it away.

"The Specialist" took extra special care of "Gerry". The world had given up on someone as severely impaired as he was. But "The Specialist" and I held an unspoken agreement to share in the responsibilities of meeting "Gerry's" needs. He bathed "Gerry" and brought him outside food - among a host of other things he needed. I tied his shoes and put on his safety helmet for him. I also watched his back during the day while he was with the other inmates.

Our relationship reached a pivotal point when I was leaving to go to the first of my series of release hearings. "Gerry" was shuffling along behind me. It was five in the morning and there he was, following me and the guards to the doorway.

"Ohhh," he said, sounding sad as the guards fastened the shackles around my ankles and hands, "My *Oobie* did something *weeally* bad." I felt my heart crumble within my chest as I tried to choke back the tears. Looking into his huge quivering eyes and seeing his uncertainty, I felt like a parent abandoning his child. I tried to make jokes to lighten the mood and make him feel better, but all he did was stand there and look at me in confusion. That day was one of the more difficult ones of my life.

"Gerry" wasn't the only love of my life. The other came in the form of a beautiful yellow Labrador named Sasha. Since the day I'd left for "The University" I was always thinking of Sasha and when I'd see her again. I missed my dog and wanted to be home again. Many nights, I'd think about how she was doing. I remember sitting in the recreation room watching Oprah on TV. She was doing a show about prison inmates who were given puppies to train for the police force. These guys were hardened criminals - murderers and thieves - not exactly the type of individuals who would be sensitive to an animal's needs. Yet, once the puppies were trained and it was time for them to be given back, these same criminals cried like babies - which shows how powerful these animals are ... and how much time I had to sit around watching Oprah.

Meanwhile, I was in the midst of trying to get released. "Johnny Cochran" had tap-danced with the State a total of six or seven years. I found myself going back and forth to court. They would come in the wee hours of the morning, put me in shackles and drag me down to the court house. Those were the worst times because that's when "Gerry" witnessed me being led away in chains, breaking my heart in two. I felt like such a disappointment to him. Deep down, I knew I would eventually be leaving him behind. I couldn't bear to think about what would happen to him once I was gone. No matter how much I hated it, that fateful day was coming - a day when I would have to look into his huge, child-like eyes and tell him I was leaving and that I wouldn't be back.

18

Free At Last

It was a battle trying to get out. Based in large part on a letter written on my behalf by one of the state forensic psychiatrists, the judge - or whoever was calling the shots - said that I was eligible for release, but couldn't leave the state without having a psychotherapist back home. This was very difficult to do. Most doctors were unwilling to take me on as a client without seeing me in person first. Others were squeamish at the idea of having a mentally ill, ex-con on their patient list. I was a huge liability. No one wanted to be held responsible if I were to somehow regress and become a danger to society on their watch. So Mom and Dad were scrambling, trying to get me a new doctor. They had no price that was too high at this point.

Mom came out to get me while Dad stayed home to work. He was pressed to the limit financially with "Johnny Cochran's" bills now coming in the mail. We needed all the money we could get to make it through this and find me a doctor.

I was released into my mother's custody and we ended up in a motel for several weeks. The people in charge told us that if I didn't get a doctor in my home state before that two-week period was up I would have to go back to TMI again. I became frantic. I missed "Gerry" and the staff members like "The Specialist" but there was no way in hell I was going back there. Mom was on her cell phone calling every doctor she could find.

Once you've been on lockdown for so long, walking around without permission feels weird and scary. I was like an animal placed in a carrying case and let loose in an unfamiliar environment. Now that I was released, I was taking my first breaths of real freedom. Freedom not only from the institution, but freedom from the paranoia and delusions as well. Every step felt brand new as I walked through the local Walmart - the central hub of the small Midwestern town we were in. The air felt fresher than I'd ever experienced it. In a sense, it was exhilarating, despite the overwhelming stress that was weighing heavily on my mother's shoulders - and mine.

The two-week deadline was fast approaching and Mom and I both knew we were running out of time. It was down to the last few phone calls when Mom found "Dr. K". A friend of the family had recommended him since she had gone through similar legal issues in the past. He agreed to take me on as a patient and now it was a dizzying rush of faxing paperwork back and forth between us, "Doc", and the State. Finally we could go home.

Dad met us at the airport with Sasha. My heart leaped as I hugged my old friend. She was a puppy when I left. Now she was huge with bright eyes, a long wagging tail and a shiny coat of flowing golden hair. I was glad to see my father, too. He looked different, older. The lines in his face spoke a thousand words - many of which were connected to sleepless nights thinking about me. But I was back in his loving arms once again after his seven year long quest to save me from myself.

Back home, I loved the familiar feelings of sleeping in my own bed, taking a hot shower without "Gerry" interrupting me – or, for that matter, just taking a shower in a private bathroom. Every morning I woke up and inhaled deeply, taking in the sweet aroma of my Mom's cooking. Life was good again.

My heart couldn't leave my friends back at TMI, though. "The Specialist" and some of the other staff were both happy and sad to see me go. I missed them. I even had their contact information. We texted sometimes and I'd send care packages to certain people. On days when I'd feel especially lonely, I'd call "The Specialist" or another staff member's cell phone. They were always happy to hear from me. They didn't see many TMI success stories. Sometimes, on these phone calls, I'd talk to my old friend, "Gerry," as well. It was always nice to hear his friendly voice.

The adjustment period was difficult and lonely. I was seeing "Dr. K" as well as working with a social worker and psychiatrist - my very own dream team. I did feel guilty about being free. Rejoining society was a constant reminder that I didn't belong there. I talked to "Dr. K" about my emotions and the things that were really going on inside my head. He was very gentle, but also pragmatic. During our sessions, he'd walk me through the pain of the past, mainly the unrequited love from my Dad while giving me another perspective to consider.

He had a way of grounding me in those moments when I was getting electrified over situations. I habitually disassociated myself from reality when the feelings of "The University" murder surfaced. There were two mes: the *me* sitting in that office - the gentle, loving soul who cared for "Gerry" and Sasha and made friends everywhere I went ... the *me* who was a little boy wanting his father's love and approval ... the *me* who watched a complete stranger plunge a knife into someone's back. Then there was the other *me* - the dark shadow ... the monster who killed another human being. That was the *me* I didn't know and didn't want to know, but would have to face if I wanted to move forward. I had to face the fact that both were *me*. I had to confront the madman who thought he was saving the world with a steak knife ... *Oh God, help me ...*

Shubi S.

The Microchip's symptoms were like a bubble that protected me from the harsh reality of what I'd done. "Doc" waited a few months before again broaching the sensitive subject of what happened. His voice was very calm and his eyes were patient and kind. The more "Dr. K" probed, the more we talked. The more we talked, the more comfortable I became with him. The more comfortable I was with him, the more candid I became. And the more candid I became, the more the bubble began losing air and deflating, leaving me without a buffer to the impact of my deeds. It all came down to one moment in his office, just the two of us seated across from each other in what started out like a typical session. That day he decided to go in deep on "the incident". Gently, he asked me what happened that day in "The University" cafeteria.

I felt myself going there with him, and the pain spread like gangrene inside my chest - a pain so deep it felt like my two lungs were full of seawater. His voice faded away to the background and there I was, floating between time and space, heaving, trying to breathe, trying to find my footing. The pain was like an out-of-body realization - so overwhelming that my mind began shutting down. Mentally, I was at the edge of a cliff, teetering, flailing my arms, knowing I was going to fall over and plunge into the unknown depths of terror. I killed this boy. A beautiful, young boy with sea blue eyes, a charming personality and a whole future ahead of him ... a boy with a family who loved him ... and a family who could no longer hold him.

From the plateau, a long, windy rope swung over the side and I gripped it feverishly with both hands. "Doctor K" saw me on the verge of a meltdown and was asking me who I was and where I was at that moment. It took me a couple of minutes to calm down, but he continued repeating my name in a firm tone, asking the same two questions over and over again until I answered him. Answering the questions made me think consciously about what he wanted to know and I began sifting my brain for the information he needed - a distraction from the internal hell my subconscious mind was putting me through. At such intense moments, he was great at throwing me a lifeline. I really needed that to help me keep in touch with reality.

Meanwhile, being free left me feeling lost and uncertain. I was isolated from my past, but unsure of the future. My neighbors and old friends - people I grew up with - only knew I was sick for a while. They could never know I killed someone and was in an insane asylum. People normally ask lots of questions - especially about people's kids - making it very difficult for my mom to discuss me in casual conversation during social encounters. My situation seemed to isolate my family from others in order to protect me.

It wasn't long until *The Man* resurfaced and began questioning what I was going to do with my future. Indian people are hard workers and my parents are no exception. They pushed through illness and all kinds of pain. No doubt *The Man* had softened up some compared to when I was younger, but it was still an unwelcome flash from the past. The difference was, this time around, I had "Dr. K" to bounce my frustrations off of. But *The Man's* words did trigger some introspection. I was an ex-con. My future was limited in the traditional respect. Getting a job was hard to do with a criminal history and, even if I got one, I was really sensitive to stress. I remembered the days slaving at the liquor store and the deli. That could never happen again.

I decided to try school one more time. I figured that was the least stressful route to take, so I applied to the local community college. At that point, I had been considering writing a book about my life, so I thought that taking an English class was the best thing to do.

Being in school again felt good. This was my third time trying to go to college. They say "three times is a charm". I guessed I would have to see. I was only going part-time with two classes, but it was still nice having a schedule again. I felt as if I was a normal, productive member of society.

Shubi S.

Compared to the recent high school graduates in my classes, I was a bit older and had lived experiences they'd only seen in the movies. Their lives seemed so different than mine, leaving me with the isolated feelings of days past.

My English class was interesting, but I spent a lot of time staring out the window daydreaming about doing more. Every day the urge was there to share what I'd been through with others. I found myself looking for more immediate ways to express my experiences in writing. I wasn't the most savvy internet person, but I managed to start up my own blog. The colleges were all using web correspondence sites for their courses - a big change since my days at "The University" and Pace. My English professor required us to log in to get updates on homework assignments and participate in online chat room discussions on something called *wordpress*.

One night, I was in the zone posting some of my thoughts on my private blog. I began telling on myself in a very big way. I typed about the murder and about serving jail time. It felt good to get it out. When I showed up to class the next day, it was cancelled. As I looked at the note on the locked door, I knew something was terribly wrong. When I got home, I called the school. They wanted to talk with my mom, so I put her on the phone. I discovered that my blog and the school forum were both on *wordpress* and I had mixed up which one was which. Now the entire class had read my personal writing. The professor was scared that I was going to come in and kill one of them. The students were scared. Everyone was afraid. They all knew about me now. It was too late.

The next thing I knew we were sitting in the dean's office. He was nice, but he didn't want me there. His exact words were: *take some time off, wait a while, and return to your curriculum later. Give this some time to blow over...* But I knew better. I'd been down this road before. I got the feeling his fingers were crossed under the desk as he was saying it.

Nevertheless, I took his advice and waited until the following semester (two or three months) and I registered for classes once again. Leery of taking English again (I had put the book idea on the back burner after last semester's fiasco) I went back to my comfort zone with a business law class and an accounting course.

My business course was a nightmare. Each class, the professor would take real-life criminal cases and use them for class discussions. Many of these class discussions revolved around people just a little too much like me. I was trying not to take it personally, but at times it seemed that my classmate's comments were passive-aggressively directed my way. I clearly remember one day where the topic was the insanity defense. We were analyzing a murder case where the person was declared not-guilty by reason of insanity. One of the kids adamantly announced to the class that anyone who kills another human being should be put away for life. The group responded in agreement and I felt very isolated and alone at that moment. Deep down, I already knew this school thing wasn't going to work. So I dropped out.

Although Mom and Dad weren't thrilled about my decision, I was happier just being honest with myself and letting things be. In one of our sessions, "Dr. K" reminded me that I was in a rebuilding process - a long, important time in my life where I needed to be completely honest with my wants, desires, and emotions. My whole downfall into madness began with trying to be something I could never be. And I couldn't afford to stress myself beyond my own threshold by living a lie again - at least if I wanted to be healthy.

19

Yesterday, Today, and Tomorrow

I can't remember when it happened, but I finally decided to be myself. I stopped trying so hard to please *The Man,* my mother, my family as a whole and society.

I also realized there are a lot of lessons that can be learned by my story. First, and this may be obvious, but you can't take back the past. No matter how much I regret and am saddened by what happened at the school, I can't change it. My mistake is something I must always live with. The effects of trauma from my crime and being locked up are there, but I am healing. I try not to think about my past or future. I just live in the moment and that keeps me happy. I am conscience and vigilant of my thoughts and behaviors. At the end of the day, I wish to be a better human being, not a more successful one. I look at life differently. My thoughts are not filled with ambition, but more with finding peace.

My father, who I demonized at times in my mind is, in fact, my biggest support and had the most positive impact on my life. He is a great provider and is nurturing. I now trust him more than my best friends. And that has healed me a lot. No, he is not perfect. He didn't have a manual on how to raise a sick child. But he succeeded. When I accomplish things in life it has a lot to do with his teachings. If I get up and give a speech, I get courage from my father.

I also learned a lot about the mental health system and its inability to help individuals in my situation. The doctors in mental health services don't spend time with patients. They get the information from second hand sources. They only see individuals when necessary or because of a crisis. For years I was assigned to a certain doctor and the best thing he ever said about me was that I was a benign patient. To me, he did not have the heart or courage to recognize that individuals with a mental illness are worth spending time with. Most professionals think we are hopeless and the hopelessness that they project on us hurts us. Conversely, if you believe in the individual and hold hope for them and give them the proper supports, recovery is possible. I'm proof of that. This is important because people with diseases should not be dehumanized. We deserve proper and good treatment as much as anyone else.

Part of that treatment is medications. And even if it means taking medicine that dulls my personality and causes weight gain, the benefits far outweigh the side effects for me. But as far as medicines are concerned, finding the correct ones for an individual is essential. The Clozaril may have treated my symptoms, but it made me a zombie. Abilify is what has worked for me with an acceptable level of side effects, but everyone is different. Also, medications are not the sole answer. There must be a complete system of support in place that is accessible to individuals when they need it, not only after they commit a crime or are in crisis. Having accessible, proper, effective and timely treatment will save lives.

That being said there is a lot of good in humanity. People are always willing to help you if you, yourself, are willing to make an effort. Tons of people in society will help you. The world is full of compassionate people who are forgiving. You just have to try to forgive yourself and make an effort to be positive.

Recovery is awesome.

Shubi S.

Finally there must be a higher power. How could there not be? Sometimes I can't believe I am still here and living. But the higher power showed mercy and grace on me.

Since I began my story with a story, I'm going to end with one, too.

This story begins when I was five years old. My mother, sister and I traveled back to India to visit the family. I remember that Dad stayed home because he had to work. We went to Old Delhi, where my mother's father lived. Like most kids in tow, I kept having to pee, but there were no public restrooms. I looked around and saw children my age defecating in the streets and begging for money or food. Mom placed her hand firmly on my shoulder and told me and my sister to keep our eyes straight and keep moving. Her parents lived in one of the nearby outskirt areas - a much better neighborhood than the inner city. Her father - we called him *Nana ji* -was very fascinating to me. Every morning he'd wake up at the crack of dawn to meditate. I'd get up, too. Sitting there next to him, watching his every move, sound, posture and facial expression, I was in awe.

Nana ji was an engineer by trade, but he was an herbal medicine-maker for the local community by passion. He was well known for his generosity and huge heart, since many of the poor would come to him and get whatever they needed without charge. Constantly, throughout the day, people would be knocking on the door asking him for medicine for their son or daughter. Depending on what the illness was, he would put together the necessary herbal concoctions and give them additional money for milk or whatever else they wanted to use it for. I remember asking him why he did that. His response was something I've never forgotten: *"that's up to God to decide if they're conning me or not ... they come to me with their problem, I have to believe them."*

Every day, I'd walk with him into town to get milk. He was a skinny guy who strolled skillfully with his cane. His sense of dignity was strong and he had an aura of discipline about him that commanded respect from everyone. In our family he was known to have paranormal abilities. Before something happened, he seemed to be able to sense it. He knew things a normal person could not possibly know. As a child, it almost sounded like he was a magical deity.

Nana ji told me a lot of stories as I sat on his lap. In Hindu religion there were many deities. He told me that he had named each one of his grandchildren after a particular god or goddess. My sister was named after the goddess of money. He named me after the god of strength. "Physical strength", *Nana ji* added thoughtfully, "not mental strength".

Later in life, I would come to realize how much power was in a name. My sister went on to become an accountant and make lots of money. I, well …was mentally weaker than my physical body, but I was indeed strong. *Nana ji's* name for me meant a lot over the years. I thought about it while in the pits of hell at "The Institution". I was strong. I could make it. It was my destiny to survive.

That visit was the only time I saw my grandfather before he died, yet, out of all the grandchildren, he left me his ring. This ring was his most prized and expensive possession. To this day I don't know why he chose me, but I believe the Universe was using its significance to show me who I really was and the lessons in life I was here to learn.

These days, I get up in the morning, walk Sasha, come back home and live the day moment to moment. Most of these moments include helping Dad out by mowing the lawn and visiting friends and family - especially my cousins. Although I wasn't up for working in any of his stores anymore, I convinced him to let me invest his money online. He was old-school and didn't have any idea about things like stocks and bonds. Grumpy and skeptical, he eventually came to trust me - especially once he saw that I didn't lose all his money and knew a thing or two about the market.

Shubi S.

Things aren't perfect. He still gets on me sometimes, but now I know it doesn't mean I'm a failure - it's just a part of the ups and downs of life. I don't have much time to dwell on it these days, anyway. I'm too busy working on my new purpose: helping others suffering with schizophrenia. I survived and they can, too. Recovery is possible. Now I travel and give speeches to help professionals understand my illness and how to help others with it. I'm also partnering with national organizations as a consultant and mentor. I've found my calling - the hard way - but I've found it. Every day new mentoring opportunities open up. The sky is the limit for what I can do. I am the man now.

MY SPEECH ON MENTAL ILLNESS AT THE POLICE ACADEMY

SEPTEMBER 2011, PENNSYLVANIA, U.S.A.

(My words verbatim and in emphasis)

I remember what a warm September day it was. I washed my face and stopped to look at myself in the mirror. Today was the beginning of the next chapter in my life.

The popular saying came to mind:

Speaking in front of crowds is the number one fear of human beings - with death being number two ... (Apparently these people have never been locked up in a mental institution).

Meanwhile, I was impressed that I got such a clean shave. Stroking my face, I was happy to see it was smooth, without any razor bumps. I pulled on my brown shirt with the button-up collar and put on my best slacks. Better hurry - I had to meet my social worker in an hour. She scheduled me for a speaking gig as part of a training seminar for police officers to work more effectively with civilians who are experiencing a mental health crisis. With my book already in the works, my dream of helping others was coming true.

I was nervous when the social worker escorted me into the huge room filled with police officers - none of who looked like me - sitting there with pads to take notes or with their arms crossed in expectation.

The next thing I knew, my name was being announced and I was standing at a podium in front of a microphone. I adjusted the mouthpiece so I could speak into it better.

Shubi S.

"Good morning. My name is Shubi ... I'm 31 - actually I just turned 32 ..."

"... and I'm a paranoid schizophrenic".

Crickets were chirping loudly. I took a deep breath and kept going.

"I encourage all of you to participate in this, and ask me questions. Make comments, whatever you want to do ... make jokes, even. Have fun with it, because ... why not? I'm not getting paid for it, so you might as well have fun".

[Small pockets of laughter came from different parts of the room. I silently breathed a sigh of relief at the sight of them warming up].

"Seriously, my story ... I'm going to keep it short. It's not really a 45-minute story - it's more like a five hour story. But I'm gonna keep it short and simple ..."

My mind was racing. Would they judge me? Would they hate me? Am I setting myself up to go back to jail? I took another deep breath. Alright, here I go ...

"Eight years ago I committed murder. Yeah, I know, a nice guy like me killing someone? It's a complicated story, but there were two incidences. One incident I stabbed a kid with a pen. He didn't die, it was a first attempt. It was at a school, and they didn't arrest me or call the cops - which was a major issue in the story, too. Later on, I committed murder - I stabbed a kid in the back ..."

"How does someone do those things when they are insane, you know? This disease affects your behavior and throws off chemicals in your brain. You can't really see the different levels of what's happening. But these chemicals really affect your actions. Some people just talk a lot of crap and say "I hate the world" or "I'm gonna kill you" and some people actually act on those feelings or behaviors".

"I feel like my disease tortured me for a long time, like ten years. It was my thoughts. No one was torturing me but myself [my own thoughts]. And that's horrible. It's a horrible way to live life."

"Yes, I feel very guilty for what I did. If I didn't feel guilty I probably wouldn't be doing this right now. I wanted to alleviate my conscience; I wanted to help/make people with mental illness have better lives, you know? That's why I'm motivated to do this."

"And responsibility is another key to my story".

"Society has that question: should this guy be responsible? How long should he be trapped or in jail? How long should he be punished-for life? For half the time? For a little bit of time? Well, I'm a law-abiding citizen now and if I respect laws, then I have a right to be free".

"With that I guess, what else can I say? I really want to talk about how the Schizophrenia has affected my life. I really want to talk about that. It affected my whole family. My family was suffering with me as I was doing stupid things and when I was homeless in the street for no reason ... things like that ... but before I talk about that, does anyone have any questions?..."

A woman raised her hand.

"When you stabbed, uh, when you did the murder, were you diagnosed with schizophrenia?"

"I had seven hospitalizations in Pennsylvania before I went to [the Midwest], so I was definitely diagnosed. But then that's another thing with my story. People will say "why didn't you just take your medicine?" -right? But I was in denial. I didn't believe I had a disease. So they would commit me for seven days and I thought that they were trying to torture me or conspire against me, that's why I was there ..."

"So did you do time?" she asked.

"Seven years."

"Seven years?"

"Yeah. The laws placed me in County Jail, then Prison hospital, and then the Institute (for mental health)."

"And that's how you got better?"

"Therapy and meds, therapy and meds."

"Are you under court order right now to take your medication?" a guy asked.

"Yeah, I see a psychiatrist once a month who writes up a report."

"So you were diagnosed as a child with this?"

"No, I was a young adolescent at the full onset of the disease".

"How old were you when you were diagnosed?" the woman asked.

"About twenty years old ... twenty one, twenty-two, maybe."

"You said you have a family, right?" the guy asked.

"Yeah".

"Do they ever wake - are they afraid of you in the middle of the night or anything like that?"

"No, no. We get along pretty good now - I mean we get along really well. I'm at peace with my family. They love me a lot. And I think they're such good parents ... I'll tell you this. They're not scared of me, but if they were scared of me, they're really an example to how parents should be because they would have me in their house anyways rather than have me locked up - that's how good parents they are. It's a lot of love between us. But they're not scared of me, they're not."

"How do you handle crowds, like going in to a mall or anything like that - are you good with that?" another guy asked.

"I was just at the mall yesterday."

"If it's like really crowded?"

"I've had some social anxiety before, but I'm getting over it with therapy and ... I'm just getting over it."

"Now what do you do if the crowds are really, really bad there?"

"I would just walk out. But that situation doesn't really affect me that much. It's more like my ... if I had the disease again it would affect me, you know? It's not a crowd thing. I'm able to sit in front of all of you and talk to you guys, so it's not so much that. I do have some social anxiety but ..."

"How long are you on this court order to take your meds?" another guy began.

"I'm not sure. It's an indefinite period of time. Indefinite."

"I see a social worker. I have a therapist once a week. Um, let's see ... a psychologist, therapist, social worker, and a court judge on a monthly basis. He will decide if I will stay out for that month. It's on a month to month basis."

"A BIG support to ME is my dog. She's sitting there on the floor. So I hang out with my dog a lot ... and dogs are really effective in therapy. I don't know if you guys know about dogs - you're police officers so I suppose you do, but she's been a big help to me. I take her for a walk every day, she never leaves me ... THAT keeps me grounded, you know? That keeps me focused and grounded. Petting the dog ... responsibility ... I mean, I love my dog ... so ... what else?"

Shubi S.

Another officer had something to say.

"When you're affected by the disease, what's going on in your mind? If we deal with someone that's affected by Schizophrenia, what can we expect? I mean, what's going through your mind? Do you feel like everyone's out to get you? Do you feel - "

"Yeah, a whole bunch of things, but I need some water first..."

Part two (my words in emphasis)

"I have hallucinations and I have delusions. They were all compounding each other at the same time. Delusions are like a misconstruction of reality. So I'm thinking I'm in the middle of a class-action lawsuit and I have to save the world. That's my delusion. My hallucinations would be about this lawsuit: What should I do? What actions should I take to win the lawsuit ...? So kill this person, commit suicide ... I was on a suicide/homicide mission, almost like a Jihad mission, okay? And then my paranoia was like, look at that person - you know, they said move your hand over here to here. I'm thinking, was that a sign that I should do something else? So there was a whole bunch of things that really affected how I was acting, you know? This disease really affected it. And I am going to write a book about it, because I can remember all these things. I think that the book should help a lot of people ... But um ... do you have any more questions?"

"I assume that's typical, then" offered another officer. "I mean you can tell the difference. Let's say a police officer showed up in uniform, would that spark it? Would that make it worse with your feelings than with a regular person?"

"That's a good question. It depends on individuals and their personal delusions. If I were delusional against police officers, then a police officer would make it worse. But I wasn't at that specific time, you know? Like I remember one time, I just had all these conspiracy theories but police were sometimes a part of it, but not if I would see them face to face. Sometimes it's different. I would be more fearful actually. [With police] there's a safety, but also a fear."

"When you were off your medication, did it consume your daily life or was it more episodic where something triggered this ... or do you lead like a "normal life" but then something triggers this? If you had a delusion about police officers and a police officer came into a store would that trigger it or something or is it something that was just constant?"

"For me it was constant. For different people like bi-polar people they have the mania and then they have this depression. I'm paranoid schizophrenic, so it's all the time. My head was hurting. The pain in my head was severe. And it was - I'd wake up in the morning and I'd be thinking about all these people who were conspiring against me. I'd drown myself in Kamu tea - didn't help. Take Tylenol, Advil - didn't help. Anything but those psychotropic medicines. You know I had a real hatred for those medicines. Not the medicine I'm currently on, because it[the other medicines] gives you all these side effects, so I thought people were trying to kill me with these medicines. And it really consumed my entire life. Every waking moment, not getting enough sleep, waking up in the middle of the night, stuff like that ... so it was torture. It was really torture. My head was hurting. You talk about wars, I feel like I'VE been through a war. I'm entitled to say that, because of the things I saw and things that happened to me delusion-wise and everything-wise ... I saw crazy stuff. It's hard to explain. It's really hard to explain."

Someone else had a question.

Shubi S.

"What were the circumstances around the kid you stabbed?"

"I didn't know him that well. I met him like once or twice and had casual conversations with him. But I thought he was the head of the conspiracy against me at that particular time. And we were in the cafeteria and I was sitting here and then moved from table to table to get closer to him just to do what I did ... and that's what happened. And I don't like getting in too much about it, but that's what happened."

"How old were you when you did that?" another guy said.

"Twenty four, I think? Twenty four."

"You ever have any concerns about driving on the highway or anything like that? Would you get some kind of episode?"

I laughed.

No, nooo - I drive all the time. I go visit my sister, I drive my parents around, and drive pretty much all the time. I know your orientation is about me and the community, but you don't need to be concerned -

"Oh, no, it's not that," The officer corrected me, "It's about your state of mind to react when you're in certain places."

"I'm a cautious driver. I don't speed. I stop at the stop signs. And I'm cautious because I'm cautious with my life, now and other people's lives ..."

"Was that different when you were off the meds?" someone else inquired.

"Sure, sure. When I was in New Holland I had this beer distributor and I took my car and was driving really fast because I thought people were following me with their cars. Yeah, that definitely would be a big difference."

"Do you have to carry anything on you to say you have this disease?"

"No. It might be a good idea to get a card or something and put it in my wallet – but no, I don't have to carry anything."

"With any kind of a disease, meds often need adjusting. Is there anything that you can now feel that you're starting to have issues with or indicate that you're going back towards that? Is there something like an early sign that you need to get to your doctor?" another officer wanted to know.

"The first symptom to go is your sleep, that's what the psychiatrist will tell you. So I try to get enough sleep and I'm careful about my sleep thing. I have a PRN ... it stands for something ... all I know is that it means "as needed" ... a drug treatment for meltdowns. My PRN is Clonafit as needed ... plus I'm already on 30 mg of Abilify. I won't have any hallucinations with Abilify, but if I get a little bit on edge I'll take Clonafit and then I'll get knocked out for a little while and kinda be sedated and be back to normal the next day."

"A lot of what we heard yesterday was that once they're on their meds patients start to feel better and they think life is good and they stop taking the meds."

"That's a common problem amongst mentally ill people. And I don't know why – see, the disease is different than Cancer or something. Because it's in the head, people have their own notions about it. A lot of people are still in denial. When you get to that stage of denial with your disease, you have to move forward and say I have this disease and I need these meds, I'm feeling good BECAUSE of the meds ... and until you do that, you're always going to relapse. The meds are really important. And some people need the adjustments, you're right. Some people don't – as much. And I have a psychiatrist that monitors me closely, a good psychiatrist. He's really perceptive, too, so it's not like a bullshit "Hey

I'm fine - I'm alive - okay bye". He asks me questions and if I need more meds, he'll just give it ... and I'll take it."

A female officer raised her hand. "As police officers when we deal with somebody when you're off your meds, how can we convince you to go get help, to take your medicine? Is there anything we can say to convince you when your family's trying to get you back on your meds and you're doing irrational things?"

"No, probably not. There's nothing you can do. When someone is going through delusions, the best thing to do - I know this sounds bad - but lock them up. That's the very best thing to do. Not lock them up in jail, lock them up in a hospital where they can take their meds, you know? I'm just speaking for myself. I'm not saying it's the best thing for everyone. If someone were to lock me up in the hospital for a long period of time, then I might have realized it ... but because of insurance ways, and other rules - like if you don't injure yourself or others for a period of time then you get released. That's bulllshit."

"That's the problem that we have. If the person didn't commit a crime and they're not a danger to society yet, THAT'S what we have a problem with as police officers and families. How do we convince the person in that interim when they're going to continue doing terrible things but they haven't yet, to get help, to get them to sign themselves into the hospital or - "

"I can't answer your question. What I can say is things sometimes run its course. It's a process, things run its course. With a disease like this, a person has to come to their own realization. Now remember the studies have shown that there's no correlation between paranoid schizophrenia and violence. So to say someone's mentally ill and they're going to commit a crime because they're mentally ill alone, it's not fair ... any other questions?"

Part three

"Are you able to work?"

"That's a good question. That's a really good question. My dad really wants me to work, and I haven't been working except trading stocks and I'm actually really good at that. And I'm writing a book ... and uh, that's the issue me and my dad are having right now, actually. I see his point of view but I also see my point of view. I'm not a lazy person, but I've been through a lot of trauma and I haven't done healing. If you tell my dad that, he's really traditional. He's like "What the hell kind of shit is this!" so I don't know. I'm able to work somewhat, but not like eight hours and that's what it is ... Anymore questions?"

"Did you have any drug and alcohol use?"

"Alcohol use. Yeah. I used alcohol. I self-medicated before my hallucinations and being hospitalized - "

"Did that seem to make you worse?"

"Probably made it worse, but temporarily it made me feel better. I drank like crazy - "

"Does it make the hallucinations worse?"

"Um ... no. When I was self-medicating I had more of a mood disorder. I wasn't having hallucinations back then."

"What kind of leisure activities do you do?"

"I walk the dog once or twice a day. Sometimes I walk with my buddies, sometimes I walk alone. I watch the CNBC Bloomberg a lot. I used to read a lot of financial magazines, which I've stopped doing. I'm more into trading on just the news and intuition and stuff. It's a very

volatile market. So, I do the market, hang out with buddies. I don't do a whole lot of recreation - stopped going to the gym because I can't get enough energy to pump iron and stuff - so I don't do that. I'm really content and peaceful in my life. I don't want to change a whole lot. My dad might send me on some silly little errands like mow the lawn, take out the trash and go see some business somewhere and I'll do that stuff. I don't know ... I'm just chillin.' Honestly, I'm just chillin'. I'm not going to harm anyone, I'm not going to harm myself, I'm just having a good time, I'm peaceful, you know?"

"Back to the question about how to deal with people that are having the episodes at the time. You said the primary goal was trying to get them to the hospital, to get them the help they need. Do you find that it helps to play along with the delusion to get what we want - the goal - instead of arguing with you? Would it be of any help to us to go along with the delusion that the people in the hospital are going to conspire with you?"

"That could be dangerous, but I don't have the answers to solve these things. I'm not a doctor"

The therapist jumped in to address it. "We will get more into that. We're actually going to role-*play*. It takes time and it's frustrating. Even professionals don't have all the answers. Every person is individual."

"You know, how you treat people is really important. There was one speaker who used to be an inmate at the Institute where I was being held and he came in to give a speech. I'll never forget his words:

"Even at my worst I still remember ... even at my worst I still remember how those people treated me - the good ones and the bad ones ..."

"That's really important in life - treating people kindly. And that may sound hypocritical of me, but I've learned the lesson, because I didn't always treat people so nicely ... "

"You talked about hanging out with your buddies. Have you been able to maintain relationships outside of your family?"

"Some, but not all. The best buddy I have is this boy named [Jesse]. He's a real nice guy. He's been my friend since we were five. Even when I was sick, he'd wake me up in the middle of the day and say 'hey, let's go, man. Let's go for a walk, let's do something - you can't just lay around in the house all day!' He's a real nice guy. He's friends with this other guy I grew up with ... doesn't he work for the police department or something? I don't know. Great guy though."

"You used a uh, kind of a hot-button word- you used the word *Jihad*."

"Oh yeah - that's part of my delusions. But I didn't mean anything by it - I'm Hindu - "

"What I mean is when you were having your delusions or your hallucinations, was *Jihad* a part of your delusion or hallucination or was that just you trying to use a word to bridge the two so we can understand what you were talking about?"

"If you read my book you'll find out - "

Once again laughter burst out in the room. However, this guy wasn't amused.

"I'm trying to find out *now*. When you're having these hallucinations as far as really towards you, so we can help you - so we can understand what you're going through. Is it real like a dream as you're standing here talking to us right now or is it reality of your experience when going through the hallucinations or the delusions?"

I had a lot of religious fixations that's really common with mentally ill people and that's why I used the word 'Jihad'. I didn't mean to offend you guys - "

"No, my question is when you're going through these experiences, is it real like we're sitting here right now or is it like a dream. To me when I'm dreaming you kinda know that it's there but you just can't determine if it's real or it's not?"

"It can be as real as us sitting here. Some people are like that. I have a lot of insight into my illness if something goes wrong. But at that time it was as real as anything that you know. But some people as they get better they can question whether it's real or not and then they can talk to people about it. But for somebody who was as sick as I was, it was absolutely 100% real for me. It's so hard for me to describe. I can only describe a little bit of what I was going through. But when you actually see something and you're hearing something, you know, it's so hard to say that's not a real thing. It's very difficult. Especially when it's happening to someone for so long.   If it's happening for, maybe like that (I snapped my fingers) then you don't really think too much about it but when it happens for years then you start believing all this stuff."

"How long have you been on medication now, since your last terrible episode that they had you put away?"

"Seven years. Seven to eight years."

"During these seven to eight years, while you're taking your medications are you still having delusions and hallucinations?"

"No, I'm not. I am not."

"So the medication you're taking is able to block out all hallucinations and delusions?"

"Yes it is, yes it is."

"While we're on the street and we're talking to someone and they're telling us that they're taking their medication we can understand that they probably aren't having delusions in the first place?"

"No, that's not always the case."

"That's where I was going-"

"It depends on the particular disease and the different individuals and depending on the medication. You can't just make that statement 'you're on your meds you're not having any problems.' Not the case. It may be less problems. It depends on the med. Maybe it's the wrong med for them. So there's a lot of factors. And some people even on several medicines still have a little bit of the delusions or hallucinations. Sometimes the voices get less, or better ... or nicer, but they don't go away. You can be on two strong anti-psychotics and she still believes she's married to God. With some people that's the best they're probably going to get."

"I hope I've helped shed some light on schizophrenia and mental illness today. That's the only objective here - my objective - and maybe a little more compassion. I know you guys are probably very compassionate people when you're dealing with those folks out there, you know? The most amount of compassion you can have, empathy is just the best, you know? That's it ... .any more questions?"

No one responded, letting me know it was time to call it a day.

Thanks, guys.

Made in the USA
Charleston, SC
01 March 2013